# INTEGRAL ECONOMY

Reforming Economic Institutions
to Serve Society

# *Advance Praise*

In *Integral Economy: Reforming Economic Institutions to Serve Society,* Gordon Anderson presents a bold vision for transforming the present U.S. centralized economy into a decentralized system. For readers willing to consider alternative economic approaches designed to preserve freedom while potentially increasing fairness, *Integral Economy* provides food for thought. The ultimate value of this book may be its insistence that we ask larger questions about the quality of our society's economic relations.

—**Steve McIntosh,** author of *Truth Emerging: A Developmental Philosophy of Purpose and Progress*

Afflicted by political corruption, economic chaos, and cultural calamity, "We the People of the United States" need new visions for a better future 250 years after the nation's founding. Gordon Anderson's *Integral Economy* takes significant steps in that direction. Brimming with challenging ideas and inviting vigorous debate, this compact book will help Americans to discern the best ways forward.

—**John K. Roth,** Edward J. Sexton Professor Emeritus of Philosophy, Claremont McKenna College. author of *Saving the American Dream: Meditations for Dark Times*

# INTEGRAL ECONOMY

## Reforming Economic Institutions to Serve Society

by

Gordon L. Anderson

PARAGON HOUSE

First Edition 2026

Published in the United States by
Paragon House
www.paragonhouse.com



Names: Anderson, Gordon L., (Gordon Louis), 1947- author.
Title: Integral economy: reforming economic institutions to serve society / by Gordon L Anderson.
Description: First edition. | [Saint Paul] : Paragon House, 2026. | Includes bibliographical references and index. |
Summary: "We need a reformation of capitalism comparable to the protestant reformation in religion. Instead of money being controlled by central banks, as religion was by the Church, each person should be economically autonomous.

An integral economy is binary. Each individual has the right to own the fruits of their labor and capital. Economically responsible individuals are nourished by ethical personal institutions on the right wing of society. The economic playing field is structured and refereed by ethical institutions on the left wing of society. Both right and left respond to a higher authority in the 'head'.

The book covers economic history, money, banking, binary economics, corporations, taxes, capital distribution, and an economic path upward for everyone. It is complete with appendices that contain five bills ready to make the U.S.. Economy integral: (1) the Decentralized Banking and Currency Stability Act; (2) the Shareholder Dividend and Corporate Tax Reform Act; (3) the Patent Reform and Public Access Act; (4) the Youth Civil Service and Economic Autonomy Act; and, (5) the Capital Income Act.."-- Provided by publisher.

Identifiers:
LCCN: 2026025996
ISBN Paper: 978-1-55778-952-5
ISBN E-book: 978-161083-135-2

The paper used in this publication meets the minimum requirements of American National Standard for Information Sciences—Permanence of Paper for Printed Library Materials, ANSIZ39.48-1984.

Manufactured in the United States of America
10 9 8 7 6 5 4 3 2 1

*I would like to acknowledge four thinkers who influenced my thought on the ideas in this book:*

*On Integral Studies:*
*Alan Combs and Ken Wilber*

*Committee on Social Thought:*
*F.A. Hayek and Edward Shils*

# Contents

**Appendices**

# List of Figures

# *Preface*

Ths book is about creating an ecnomic system that serves individuals in their pursuit of life, liberty, and happiness and serves society as a whole. It follows several other books I have written on the historical developments that led to the U.S. Constitution, its successes, and the developments that enabled special interests to hijack or circumvent the system, inhibiting individuals' pursuit of life, liberty, and happiness today.

In *Philosophy of the United States: Life, Liberty, and the Pursuit of Happiness* (2004), I described the U.S. founding as the creation of a governance framework that facilitated the rights and ideals in the Declaration of Independence. Many of the founders were fluent in Latin and Greek and understood the successes and failures of the Greek City States, the Roman Republic, and the Roman Empire.

The Protestant Reformation had declared the sovereignty of individuals in their relationship to God and each person's responsibility for their own life. This led people to demand control over their own governments. In addition to the lessons of ancient Greece and Rome, the founders were influenced by recent and contemporary thinkers such as Adam Smith, David Hume, John Locke, and Baron de Montesquieu (Charles-Louis de Secondat).

The Constitution was intended to establish a level playing field and guardrails that would allow individuals to pursue their lives freely. While the First Amendment had separated religious institutions from the state, other institutions were used to hijack the government. In his Farewell Address, George Washington lamented that political parties and factions exerted too much influence. Then came corporations with their lobbying power. This was followed by the Federal Reserve and bureaucratic federal agencies doling out money to the states, turning a union of self-sufficient states into an empire with economically dependent states.

I wrote *Life, Liberty, and the Pursuit of Happiness, Version 4.0* (2009) after the economic collapse of 2008. This book outlined five necessary principles of governance that were intended at the founding but have been increasingly violated as special interests found ways to game the system. These principles are: (1) protection, (2) subsidiarity, (3) separation of function, (4) transparency, and (5) the right to secede. The existing government was examined against these five principles, with policy suggestions for restoring them in the conclusion.

In 2009, the late Alan Combs arranged for me to teach a course on Integral Society at the California Institute of Integral Studies. *Integral Society: Social Institutions and Individual Sovereignty* (2023) was indebted to the philosophy of Combs, Ken Wilber, and F. A. Hayek, and others. It provides an updated Declaration of Independence, not just from the British Crown, but from all social institutions used to manipulate, control, and exploit the individuals they should serve. It proposes an updated constitutional framework for an integral society in which institutions across all three social spheres and at all social levels function as organs of the body, serving sovereign individuals and the whole of society.

This book, *Integral Economy: Reforming Institutions to Serve Society,* examines how economic institutions can be transformed to make the economy, and the entire society, more integral. The Protestant Reformation wrested individuals free from the monopoly of the Church. Modern Constitutional Republics gave individuals a political voice and freedom from the arbitrary rule by kings. However, no comparable development has occurred where individuals have been freed from centrally controlled economies with central banks like the U.S. Federal Reserve. Reforms are necessary for economic institutions to support the economic sovereignty of individuals, decentralizing control over wealth. This book explains that an integral economic system can be based on the assets of all individuals—a system in which the central bank will own nothing and be happy.

# Introduction: Integral Economy

Societies have become much more complex since modern nation-states emerged in the 17th century. Rational, impersonal, and bureaucratic social institutions have replaced the arbitrary rule of individuals. Corporations, central banks, political parties, government bureaucracies, universities, and other impersonal institutions have displaced the rule by kings, popes, and feudal lords. These institutions can give individuals greater freedom and opportunity to pursue happiness, or they can become instruments of structural oppression. This depends on their purpose, design, and management.

In my previous book, *Integral Society: Social Institutions and Individual Sovereignty,* I explained that social institutions exist at different levels of society (e.g., family, community, city, state, world) and in three major spheres (e.g., culture, governance, and economy). In an integral society, social institutions work together harmoniously, serving both individual happiness and the well-being of society as a whole.

The Renaissance and the Reformation transformed the feudal society, where most people were agricultural serfs and peasants, to one in which individuals could earn an independent living as craftsmen, merchants, and tradespeople in cities. The Protestant Reformation promoted the belief that each individual is ultimately accountable to God, not to churches, priests, or popes. Widespread education was facilitated by the printing press, which made it possible for everyone to read the Bible and other literature. Individuals did not have to rely on the word of authorities to become active social agents. This led to the desire for political autonomy and self-rule under democratic and republican institutions of governance.

The rise in individual freedom and autonomy unleashed developments in science, technology, and industry that created vast wealth and a comfortable living for those with ingenuity, a strong work ethic, and financial discipline. Top-down social institutions were replaced by the bottom-up creation of social institutions designed to serve sovereign individuals. Institutions created to rule people were replaced by institutions designed to serve people. But many of these institutions were soon hijacked and misused.

Ancient political philosophers like Aristotle discussed good and bad kings. Good kings served the people and helped them to prosper and pursue happiness, while bad kings were tyrants who used the people for their own wealth and happiness. Today, we need to study what makes modern social institutions good or bad, whether their purpose, structure, and management is an ethical or unethical framework that serves all individuals or provides a few leaders with extraordinary power and wealth. Centralized institutions and monopolies tend to serve elites, while decentralization, voluntary membership, and competition among institutions tend to serve individuals' freedom and autonomy.

## Cultural Institutions and Individual Sovereignty

In the Holy Roman Empire, the Catholic Church had a monopoly on culture, control of ancient texts, history, education, and social norms. The Pope and the hierarchy below him promoted "official truth" as dogma, for better or worse. People were expected to believe and obey what they taught, even if it caused them harm. Those who opposed the official dogma were often killed, and their writings burned. These were called "dark" ages because the light of new truth was unable to shine. However, the values promoted by the Church were a check on the behavior of the kings and princes, who were also expected to serve God and the good.

In 1517, Martin Luther spoke out against the abuses of power and hypocrisy of the leadership after visiting Rome and witnessing lavish lifestyles of the papal hierarchy. His 95 theses challenged the universal authority of the Catholic Church, and created cognitive dissonance among believers and rulers, who were forced to decide who to believe.

In 1530, Henry VIII, who had opposed Luther in England, broke from the Roman Catholic Church when it forbade his divorce from Cathrine of Aragon. The new Church of England remained a top-down institution that served the power of the state. This check on the behavior of the King was removed when there was no longer a cultural standard on divorce.

The breakdown of the Catholic Church's monopoly on culture, combined with more widespread reading and education, led to decades of war and confusion over religious truth and the bottom-up formation of religious sects and churches following evangelists and theologians. Most Baptist, Congregationalist, and United Church of Christ churches are locally organized communities. Many independent Evangelical, Pentecostal, and non-denominational churches focus on personal spiritual nurture and autonomy.

Many official state churches, like the Lutheran churches in Scandinavia, remain. However, the priests in state churches are not as motivated to compete for members as evangelical churches. When priests' salaries are paid by the state, they do not focus on winning converts or nurturing souls, but on performing the required ceremonial services. The search for new truth falls outside the church and into the private sector.

In the United States, the First Amendment forbade the establishment of a state religion, yet religion flourished more than in Europe. Churches have to serve both the spiritual and ceremonial needs of members, or they will go out of business. Those that provide spiritual nourishment flourish while others decline.

When the state has excessive control over religion, whether Christianity or another religion, people are unable to speak openly, and other means of cultural enrichment, even joining underground movements. Even though mosques in Iran are legally organized like non-profit churches in the U.S., the control of the state by clerics leads to the same result. People are not nourished by political rhetoric, disguised as religious teaching. So far in the 21st century, 50,000 of the 75,000 Iranian mosques have closed because of this.[1] Christianity grew rapidly in home meetings despite state repression.[2]

1. https://allarab.news/50000-mosques-have-closed-in-iran-are-iranians-seek-truth-outside-of-islam/

2. https://persecution.org/2023/07/20/the-worlds-fastest-growing-church/

People want to search for, understand, and live truth in their pursuit if happiness. They want cultural autonomy, the ability to pursue new truth, and to determine their personal identity. Dogma is repulsive to the normal process of maturity. When religious institutions are hijacked and fail to serve the spiritual and cultural needs of individuals, they become obstacles to an integral society. Organic cultural institutions are still rare. Political and economic interests continually co-opt them. However, there is increasing pressure by individuals to replace leader-controlled institutions with those run by members and serve individuals' needs.

## Governance Institutions and Individual Sovereignty

Modern political theory begins with Thomas Hobbes (1651),[3] who argued that sovereign individuals could create a social contract that directs the ruler's duties. The ruler legally works for the people. The social contract makes the ruler an administrator of people's laws rather than a king or dictator who makes his own laws. To keep the ruler from becoming a dictator, the contract has to be enforced by institutional checks and balances on power. These checks and balances reached maturity in Montesquieu's *Spirit of the Laws* (1748).

The U.S. Founders drew on Montesquieu and others when designing the U.S. Constitution. However, John Adams warned that this governance system "was made only for a moral and religious people. It is wholly inadequate to the government of any other."[4] In a government of the people, the people must be able to govern themselves individually, and also have ethical institutional frameworks. The Judeo-Christian tradition teaches principles of personal self-governance but says little about rational, impersonal, social institutions. In an integral society, individuals need to be guided by an "integral consciousness" that includes both.[5] This consciousness is necessary to function as a culturally autonomous

3. Thomas Hobbes *Leviathan* (NY: Macmillan, 1962).

4. President John Adams, Letter to Officers of the First Brigade of the Third Militia of Massachusetts, October 11, 1798.

5. See, Ken Wilber, *A Theory of Everything* (Boston: Shambhala, 2001), p. 21ff.

adult in a society of complex and ethical institutions. Ken Wilber, a pioneer in integral theory, considered many of the U.S. Founders to display an integral consciousness when establishing the Constitution for the new government.[6]

American history shows the truth of John Adams' statement. Leaders have engaged in power-grabbing, cronyism, vote-buying, and selling their office for wealth. The Constitution gave the people ultimate power to remove such people by voting them out. However, this is difficult when citizens lack the integrity to vote for righteous leaders who reveal an integral consciousness, and instead vote for those who pander to a lower consciousness.

The tension between individuals who want a voice in governance and those who want the government to care for them as children is pronounced. However, the idea of sovereign individuals controlling their government is gradually gaining traction around the world. Most modern constitutions declare the people sovereign, even though elites use social institutions to suppress that sovereignty.

## Economic Institutions and Individual Sovereignty

We have discussed bottom-up institutions in both the cultural and governance spheres. However, the economic sphere remains centrally controlled through central banks and government cabals. Economic institutions have not yet devolved power to the people. As Friedrich Hayek observed:

> The great trouble is that money wasn't allowed to develop. After two or three hundred years of the use of coins, governments stopped any further developments. We were not allowed to experiment on it, so money hasn't been improved; it has rather become worse in the course of time.... What we have had since was mostly government abuses of money.—F. A. Hayek.[7]

6. Ibid., p. 90.
7. Friedrich A. Hayek. Interview by James U. Blanchard III, May 1, 1984. Cato Institute Policy Report May/June 1984. https://www.cato.org/policy-report/may/june-1984/exclusive-interview-fa-hayek#.

We have many examples of individual economic autonomy based on individual labor. As we mentioned, the tradesmen and merchants in late medieval European towns and cities became economically self-sufficient from their own labor. At the time of the U.S. founding, the economy was largely democratic, based on individual labor in family farms and businesses that created self-sufficient communities. R.H. Tawney wrote in *Protestantism and the Spirit of Capitalism* (1926) that the drive for personal autonomy and a hard work ethic was instilled into the consciousness of protestants. They exhibited great economic productivity and personal success. The opportunity for individuals to pursue economic autonomy in the United States, with the ability to own a farm or start a business, led to mass migration from Europe.

In early America, the economy approximated economic democracy. The theories of Adam Smith in *An Inquiry into the Nature and Causes of the Wealth of Nations* (1776) and *The Theory of Moral Sentiments* (1759) applied to this situation. The labor-based economy enabled everyone to enjoy the fruits of their labor. This was a pre-capitalist economy, when many people could live with little or no money.

In early America, corporations were viewed with distaste, and the Hudson's Bay Company and East India Company left. Banks primarily served overseas trade merchants. There was little institutional lending to average citizens. Many stores had personal credit accounts that could be settled when crops or goods were sold. Personal and family lending was common. Impersonal economic institutions were undeveloped.

The U.S. Founders were heatedly divided over a national bank. Alexander Hamilton wanted a national bank to support national industry, while Thomas Jefferson, James Madison, and later Andrew Jackson were strongly opposed to such economic centralization, considering it unconstitutional and the basis of tyranny. They preferred state-chartered banks.

Hamilton pushed a charter for the First National Bank through a divided Congress in 1791, but in 1811, the majority of Congress viewed it as unconstitutional and did not renew it. In 1816, the Second National Bank was chartered to help address wartime financing problems. In

1832, President Andrew Jackson considered it unconstitutional, vetoed its renewal, and removed all federal deposits. During the Civil War, the National Banking Acts of 1863–64 created a system of national banks that issued uniform banknotes backed by federal bonds. The creation of a central bank was staved off until 1913, when the Federal Reserve was created.

American corporations also took decades to develop and exert great economic influence on Congress. They rapidly expanded with the development of railroads, steel, and heavy industry in the middle of the 19th century. Today, the production of goods based on capital-intensive corporations greatly outstrips that produced by individual labor. However, only a small portion of the population receives the majority of the income from capital ownership. While the problem is the unethical distribution of income from capital, many promote the idea that capitalism itself is evil.

## The Lack of an Integral Institutional Economy

This introduction concludes that there has been more progress in freeing individuals from centralized religious and political institutions than from centralized economic institutions, even though an integral understanding of social institutions in general remains in its infancy. In an integral society, individuals need freedom, autonomy, and accountability in all three social spheres.

The US founders designed a constitution that checked the power of central political institutions and separated religion from the state. They did not significantly separate the political and economic institutions because they did not exist until decades later, although President George Washington lamented that they had failed to sufficiently check the influence of political parties and factions that hijacked political power.

The lack of integral economic institutions causes political and cultural dysfunction by exerting enormous economic control over cultural and political institutions that should remain dedicated to serving sovereign individuals. Reforms that make the economy integral are necessary for a healthy and functional society. We must understand what is unethical and dysfunctional in the economic systems before we rewrite or pass laws to make the economy integral.

The major problem in modern economic systems relates to the replacement of labor by capital-intensive tools and machines in the production of economic goods. Capital-intensive, impersonal economic institutions are replacing segments of the economy based on individual labor in the 18th century. This economic system, which Karl Marx named "capitalism," creates high levels of economic output that can make a better life possible for everyone. However, political and economic institutions create unethical frameworks for the distribution of capital profits, enabling a few owners to profit immensely while workers often earn a subsistence income.

The Communism that Marx proposed as an alternative was a failure, because it gave political leaders control over the economy. This is similar to Henry VIII taking control of the Church and eliminating a check on his own behavior. State churches remove the vibrancy of individuals pursuing truth in religion, and state economies remove incentives for individuals to produce. People produce to have economic autonomy, not to be dependent. Communism has everywhere led to reduced levels of production of the things people want, and forced people to produce things political leaders want, like weapons and tools of oppression.

The current centralized capitalist system will not be improved by giving more economic control to the state, but by distributing its ownership among the people. An integral economy requires a decentralized money system with equal opportunity for all individuals to receive income from the ownership of capital. No modern state has an integral economy, but there are historical experiences we can use to frame ethical economic institutions.

These experiences include lessons from medieval Italian banking, the ledger system used by the Bank of Amsterdam, and the concept of fractional reserve banking. Anti-trust laws at the end of the 19th century and banking reforms under Franklin Delano Roosevelt show that it is possible to overcome the political pressure of centralized economic institutions and have citizens force reforms through Congress. Tools for decentralizing the centralized economic institutions exist. However, strong political will and citizen education are necessary to overcome the stranglehold that unethical institutions have on the current system.

An economic parallel to the decentralization of religious and government institutions is necessary. In an integral society, responsible individuals are the backbone of the economy, and impersonal economic institutions are servants and referees. The people are the owners. The jingle associated with the World Economic Forum (WEF) is turned on its head: "Social institutions will own nothing and be happy."

## The Nature of Individuals and Institutions

Individuals are subjective moral agents. Human beings have sense perceptions and brains with consciousness that drives their actions. The ethical problem is whether these subjective actions are good or bad. People are born dependent on their parents and communities. They are takers, living off of providers. When they grow up, they become providers. The socialization process brings people from dependence to independence, becoming positive moral agents who contribute to the welfare of others and society as a whole.

This socialization process is the basis of civilization. Traditionally, personal social institutions, with the family at the center, were responsible for the socialization of individuals. Modern impersonal social institutions need to support this socialization to be ethical frameworks of society.

In the economic sphere, individual economic autonomy, productivity, and ethical behavior are needed for sustainable economic institutions. There is no coercion or theft when responsible adults voluntarily care for dependents—children, the elderly, disabled, and unsocialized individuals from their own resources. Personal institutions and impersonal institutions are integral when they promote the highest standards of conscientiousness and productivity in individuals, who are the cells of society.

The role of government is to referee the playing field of society. It enforces fair laws that allow individuals to pursue their goals, while providing guardrails that take players off the field and into a penalty box when they harm others. In the economic sphere, this means theft in any form, whether direct or indirect, needs to be prevented and punished. The government should step in when parents and schools have failed to produce ethical, subjective individuals.

Institutions do not have a conscience. They are tools designed to serve a purpose with a structure that guides that purpose. Institutions of governance are based on power, which a referee needs to do its job. Institutions of culture transmit information, values, and behavioral norms to individuals. Economic institutions facilitate the ownership, production, and distribution of goods that people need to be healthy and happy. Schools, government agencies, and banks each have a role in their social sphere, but they do not have a conscience. They are structural frameworks that can be ethical or unethical tools.

This book focuses on economic institutions and explains their relationship to cultural and governance institutions. It describes the principles and social structures that can serve the economic autonomy of ethical individuals and the integral well-being of society as a whole. In an integral economy, all individuals should have the opportunity to earn an income from both the fruits of their labor and their capital.

People should own their institutions. They own their culture through socialization and the pursuit of truth. They own governments through a vote for their representatives, who are constrained by an ethical framework with checks and balances. They own corporations as individual shareholders who receive a share of the profits that are not pilfered by holding companies, state taxes, or other unethical strategies.

## Reforming Current Economic Institutions

An integral economic system does not require a total reboot or economic revolution as Marxism-Leninism advocated. That causes the deaths of millions of innocent individuals. In the transformation to an integral economy, no one needs to die or lose personal wealth—even if they got rich by gaming unethical institutions. We do not redistribute what people have or otherwise take any wealth that people have now. Rather, rules should be changed to make the economic institutions and playing field ethical moving forward.

We can't undo the past, but people who gained wealth unethically through an unethical framework will need to play by new, fairer rules like everyone else going forward. Wealth inequalities will be gradually reduced. Zero-sum economic frameworks, where some gain at the expense of others, will end, being replaced by a positive-sum economic system. Laws that centralize new wealth need to be replaced by laws that decentralize and widely distribute new wealth. More people need to receive income from the ownership of capital, in addition to their labor.

Transformation to an integral economy does not require getting rid of the U.S. dollar or returning to a gold standard. Rather, we need to stop creating fiat or "counterfeit" money. An integral economy does not require ending fractional-reserve lending; it is a natural engine of economic expansion. However, the interest earned on fractional-reserve lending should be distributed to individual savings accounts used to back the loans, rather than saying banks own that money. An integral economy does not need to end the central printing of money, but the printing must become ethical and distributed by an agency that is a banking referee, not a player like the current Federal Reserve. In short, unethical frameworks must be transformed to ethical frameworks.

The government, like any other social institution, should be funded by the people through their representatives' legislation, not by the imposition of debt, unethical taxes, or printing counterfeit money. The Constitutional requirement that taxes be apportioned among the states met this integral principle. Tariffs and user fees, where individuals can choose whether to buy products, are not a direct confiscation of wealth. The US Founders created a more integral economic framework than we have today. The national government should be forced to balance its books just as state governments are. A core principle is that the entity that referees the money should not be able to use it, but be paid wage labor like other workers. As referees, governments need to maintain ethical guardrails on financial institutions, so that they serve their clients rather than treating clients' wealth as their own.

Patent law is also an area that requires ethical reform in an integral economy. Patents are important incentives to invent, invest in, and produce new products. However, their purpose was not to enable price gouging or withholding good products from consumers. Patents can easily be reformed to provide a windfall to inventors, while enabling good products to reach consumers at a reasonable price.

In *Integral Society,* I proposed updating the U.S. Constitution to place checks and balances on social institutions and processes that did not exist, or were in their infancy, at the time of the Founding. The left wing has attempted to use the state to centrally organize society, rather than to serve individuals' pursuit of happiness. Whether by constitutional boundaries or by laws that make existing institutions ethical, governments should become better referees and be forbidden from being players. This book outlines the reform and creation of economic institutions to achieve an integral economy.

## Outline of this Book

### Part 1: Framework for an integral economy

Chapter 1 discusses the development of economic concepts important for an integral economy: private property, virtue, market principles, capitalism, Marx's critique, binary economics, money as a spontaneous order, and social institutions as objective ethical frameworks.

Chapter 2 presents a philosophical framework and diagrams representing an integral society and economy. It describes the three pillars of society: its two wings and the head that engage in and guide social relationships. The right wing refers to personal institutions like family and community. The left wing refers to impersonal social institutions like the state, and the head contains the integral knowledge that guides both wings and the relationships in society.

## Part 2: Money and Banking

Chapter 3 discusses wealth and money, focusing on individual wealth metrics rather than GDP. It explains that some forms of money have intrinsic value, some representative value, and others an accounting unit value. It shows how fractional-reserve lending underpins the seamless expansion of the money supply.

Chapter 4 provides the framework for an integral banking system, explains why current systems are unethical, and shows how the present system can be reformed. The most important changes are: central banks becoming money referees rather than players; banking being limited to correspondent banks; and depositors owning money rather than banks. It also describes a system in which governments are forced to balance budgets without printing money. It proposes a bill that would transform the central bank into a central ledger authority.

## Part 3: Corporations and Shareholding

Chapter 5 discusses an ethical framework for corporations. This includes ownership of corporate shares and dividend payments, equal opportunity for everyone to own shares, the importance of corporate distributions of dividends to shareholders, and the need for governments to stop taxing corporate profits. It proposes a bill that ends direct taxation of corporations and mandates a percentage of profits be distributed as dividends.

Chapter 6 presents an integral framework for stockbrokers and other financial services involved in capital ownership and distribution. It distinguishes between personal institutions on the economic playing field and impersonal institutions that must serve as referees.

Chapter 7 explains patents, the problems of price-gouging and shelving, and proposes legal reforms that could eliminate these problems while still providing patent holders with financial rewards for their inventions. A patent reform act is proposed.

## Part 4 The Integral Distribution of Wealth and Capital

Chapter 8 explains taxes on income and inheritance. It emphasizes a new focus on a capital income stream through dividends more than speculation on capital gains, and the importance of taxing wage income and capital income at the same rate.

Chapter 9 argues that taxes should be on economic transactions on the playing field of society, and not on the pillars that hold it up. This means sales, income, and other taxes imposed when money changes hands, not on institutions or personal wealth.

Chapter 10 examines the importance of an upward economic path for everyone. It begins by presenting Erik Erikson's eight stages of psychosocial development, which show how individuals become productive, responsible, caring, and wise. These are the people society needs for productive social and economic relations. It next examines current programs known as "baby bonds," and argues that a Youth Civil Service program would be a better way for governments to help prepare youth for the labor market. Then it presents a modification of the baby bonds idea that would provide capital income accounts at birth, based on treasury credit, to create an IRA-type investment account. This would enable very poor people to become "trust fund babies," rather than limiting such opportunities to the super-rich.

Chapter 11 summarizes how the reforms we have proposed would help produce an integral economy. On the left, reforms of economic institutions and taxes would create a level playing field and opportunities for everyone. On the right, the government could assist in providing an economic path upward for all--both in terms of labor and capital- instead of welfare traps and dependency. This provides a society in which individuals are free to pursue happiness, while society sees steady economic development.

# Part 1

## A Framework for an Integral Economy

*For Edward Shils , editor of* Minerva, *and with whom I worked on reforming Liberal Societies.*
*Image courtesy of, and assistance by, Grok AI*

When philosophy paints its grey in grey, then a shape of life has grown old. By philosophy's grey in grey it cannot be rejuvenated but only understood. The owl of Minerva spreads its wings only with the falling of the dusk.

—G.W.F. Hegel in the Preface to his *Elements of the Philosophy of Right* (1820/1821), in a standard English translation (S.W. Dyde, 1896)

# Chapter 1

## Historical Antecedents

The historical development of economic theory reveals the outline of an integral economy. The giants in economic theory, from Aristotle to Friedrich A. Hayek, have recognized the importance of widely distributed ownership of wealth and economically responsible citizens. On the other hand, from mercantilism to the World Economic Forum (WEF) we have seen state and economic institutions concentrating wealth and inhibiting the individual pursuit of happiness.

Karl Marx was angered by this concentration of wealth, but promoted the seizure and redistribution of wealth, which destroyed individuals' incentive to produce and left them impoverished. The idea that a transition to personal economic autonomy through the dictatorship of the proletariat was fictitious and naive, as concentrated power is even more tyrannical than the concentration of wealth. In an industrial economy, Marx's unitary labor theory of value must be replaced by a binary theory of value where individuals receive income from both labor and capital.

### Aristotle and Private Property

Aristotle explained why ownership of property is essential for happiness in his critique of Plato's communism in the *Republic:*

> There is an immense amount of pleasure to be derived from the sense of ownership; every man bears love towards himself and I am sure nature meant this to be. Selfishness is condemned and rightly so, but

> selfishness is not simply love of self but excessive love of self. So excessive greed to acquire property is to be condemned, though every man, we may be sure, likes to have his bit of property. And there is this further point: there is great pleasure in giving, helping friends and associates, making things easy for strangers; and this can only be done by someone who has property of his own.[1]

Aristotle recognized the importance of economic autonomy and serving others in the pursuit of happiness. The Ancient Greek economy was based on households and small city-states. He opposed selfishness, money lending for interest, and excessive wealth accumulation, recognizing that great disparities in wealth are socially destabilizing. Though Aristotle didn't think democracy is the best form of government, he said that the best economic system for a democracy was agrarian, where everyone owned property and earned a living from their own farm or business. Such people are self-sufficient and uninterested in using the government to redistribute wealth.

## Cicero and Moral Virtue

In the Roman Republic, Cicero's views were pragmatic and addressed a larger economy with commercial interests that expanded state infrastructure and urban development. The Romans did not have access to Aristotle's texts, but shared his concerns about personal greed, justice, and the common good. Roman ethics were guided by Stoicism, which focused on moral duties in public and private life. Wealth was acceptable as long as it was acquired honestly and used virtuously. It was a virtue not to use the state for personal profit; public money was a sacred trust. Cicero defended private property ownership, and considered redistribution schemes harmful. Wealth can serve virtue and the common good. Economic calculations should include an ethical component.

In the ancient world, individuals, not institutions, managed money, and the economy was not a separate field of study, but an aspect of how

1. Aristotle, *Politics*, trans. T.A. Sinclair (Middlesex, England: Penguin, 1962), pp 63-64.

individuals behaved virtuously. This is classical Western teaching. In the 17th and 18th centuries, a complete British education included reading Greek and Latin texts. Cicero's *De Officiis* (On Duties) was taught at Eton, Winchester, Westminster, Oxford, and Cambridge to produce well-rounded aristocrats capable of leadership, public service, and prudent management of family property.

## Mercantilism as State Control of Wealth

Mercantilism is a loose set of economic policies related to state control of wealth. It developed in the 16th to 18th centuries as nation-states emerged. Kings centralized and hoarded wealth in the form of precious metals, such as the Spanish plunder of gold from the Americas. Mercantilism included state-controlled monopolies, high tariffs, and subsidies for exports. Colonialism was a result, as colonies were exploited as suppliers of resources and as captive markets. Strong navies protected these activities, which could be called government greed.

The major proponents of mercantilism were Jean-Baptiste Colbert, French minister of finance under King Louis XIV of France, and Thomas Mun, a director of the East India Company. Their writings were the economic form of Machiavelli's *The Prince,* suggesting strategies to increase state wealth.

Mercantilist policies persist today in economic debates over protectionism, tariffs, trade surpluses, central banks, and claims to natural resources. Today, the use of states' power to exploit capitalist institutions to centralize wealth is a continuation of mercantilism's use of state power in the colonial period. Adam Smith largely rejected mercantilism's core assumptions in favor of comparative advantage and mutual gains from trade.

## Adam Smith, Father of Modern Economic Theory

Adam Smith is considered the father of modern economic theory, and we might add, of integral economy. His investigations into human society led to a unified science of political economy. This meant the systematic integration of the traditional household economy, agriculture, industry, and commerce.

In *The Theory of the Moral Sentiments,* Smith, like Cicero, argued that social order becomes possible by controls that individuals place upon themselves. These controls involve individuals knowing and actualizing rules of justice and morality. It is important that others in society ensure that the inculcation and embodiment of these rules occur. Education is the responsibility of significant others in cultural institutions. The discernment required for positive moral agency includes a complex mix of sympathy, imagination, reason, and reflection.[2]

In *The Wealth of Nations,* Smith distinguished between three distinct features of production: land, labor, and capital. They corresponded to three types of monetary return: rent, wages, and capital. These three types of value provide the main elements of Smith's economic model.[3] Smith saw the spirit of monopoly in manufacturers and merchants as an extension of mercantilism's zero-sum policies. Competition and economic liberty were needed to curb this behavior.

In his theory of economic incentive, Smith modified the traditional view of "selfishness," saying it is natural to seek to acquire the necessities to live. Providing for oneself and one's happiness is not selfish or evil, but a social good insofar as it relieves others from having to provide welfare. Moral actions become bad when they harm others.[4] Thus, selfishness or greed would include using institutions to concentrate capital or control markets in ways that harm others' pursuit of economic autonomy and happiness. Following Cicero, Smith argued that an individual's use of wealth requires a sense of responsibility to others, who should be treated justly and with magnanimity.

Smith argued that the basic laws of the market—supply, demand, and competition—coupled with moral individuals who are incentivized by natural drives, the ownership of property, and free market exchange will

---

2. Andrew Skinner, "Introduction," Adam Smith's *The Wealth of Nations* (Great Britain: Chaucer Press, 1978), pp. 16-17.

3. Ibid., pp. 43-44.

4. Ibid., p. 44.

lead to prosperity and great abundance. This will be the visible product of an "invisible hand." Smith the most efficient and productive economy, with the greatest distribution of wealth, would have the maximum the number of individuals competing on a free and open economic playing field.

## Karl Marx's Critique of Capitalism

Marx studied Adam Smith and David Ricardo, saying that they correctly identified labor as the source of value, placing political economy on "firm objective foundations." But, Smith spoke of labor as the value of a product in precapitalist times, with industrial society producing wealth with capital. Marx, following Ricardo, mistakenly grounded value in a capitalist economy in labor, rather than seeing two contributors to value of a product—labor and capital.

Marx acknowledged Smith's pioneering a scientific approach to political economy. He agreed that capitalism unleashed massive productive forces and that mercantilism left this increased wealth in the hands of elites and not returned to the workers. But he considered Smith to be a brilliant bourgeois thinker who revealed capitalism's laws—yet who remained trapped in the system. He used Smith's tools to expose the existing capitalist exploitation, but failed to produce a superior economic theory. The Communist Manifesto was filled with proletarian anger against the capitalists, promoting class warfare to overthrow the capitalist system and a utopia ushered in by "the dictatorship of the proletariat" followed by the "withering away of the state."

Marx's ideas fueled revolutions worldwide. His description of the alienation and exploitation of workers resonated widely with existence of great disparities in wealth. A promised Communist utopia deceptively lured many idealists. But his naive view of social institutions, reduced to class instruments, ignored their real value as vehicles to assist the natural individual pursuit of economy autonomy. Ignoring the biological and social realities of human nature, he saw the state as creating a "new man" solely motivated by rational economic justice. He failed to understand that impersonal social institutions can have their own dynamics of power and wealth that must be checked. The state should not be an instrument of rational control that replaces the traditional institutions of family and community, but an ethical framework in which family and community play a crucial role in raising virtuous individuals, and in which guardrails are applied to the monopolistic and mercantilist abuses of capitalism, and the ownership and profits from capitalist corporations become decentralized and widespread.

Marx was a reductionist, who taught that economic conditions are the primary determinant of consciousness. While they impact consciousness, they do not fully determine it. In an integral view, there are three social spheres that contribute to individual consciousness: cultural, economic, and governance. The cultural and political spheres are not a "superstructure" built on the economic sphere as Marx taught, but separate components that each contribute to an integral society. The class warfare promoted by Marx can be viewed as a form of tribal consciousness, which is zero-sum thinking.

Adam Smith was a more integral thinker, seeing individuals' consciousness tied to biological, social, and economic needs, as rooted in much more than economic class consciousness. However, he was more traditional in his emphasis on ethical individuals rather than ethical impersonal institutions like corporations and states, which contribute to the structure of modern societies in which people cooperatively own their states, churches, and economic institutions.

The cooperative ownership of capitalist corporations, with higher quantities of production and capital income than individuals, requires more than the ethical behavior of individuals. It requires the ethical structure of capitalist institutions and laws that govern them. This requires binary economics.

## Louis Kelso and Binary Economics

An integral economy must consider labor and capital as distinct contributions to the production of goods and services. Binary economics provides a basis for the ethical use of capital ignored by both liberal and conservative economists. Louis Kelso proposed the core ideas of binary economics in *The Capitalist Manifesto,* co-authored with philosopher Mortimer J. Adler (1958). Economist Robert Ashford explains,

> Binary Economics offers a conception of economics that is foundationally distinct from the economic theories presently employed by government, private enterprise, charitable institutions, and individuals to formulate and evaluate economic policy.[5]

Louis Kelso wrote:

> (1) labor and capital are equally fundamental or "binary" factors of production, (2) technology makes capital much more productive than labor, (3) the more broadly capital is acquired with the earnings of capital, the faster the economy will grow.[6]

Adam Smith wrote about three factors of value: land, labor, and capital. Kelso considered land and other natural resources as capital, using a wider definition of capital than Smith. The core problem to address is the concentrated ownership of any capital, whether in the form of natural resources, property, money, shares in corporations, or other economic goods.

Kelso noted that labor accounted for 95 percent of economic production in 1776, when the U.S. was founded. In the North, most of the population owned farms, shops, or practiced trades in which all of their income came from their labor. Fewer than 2 percent of the population in the North were slaves. The South had a different economy. It was still based on labor, but human beings were exploited, as in the colonialist tradition of mercantilism.

This labor-based economy in the North approximated economic democracy because nearly everyone had economic autonomy and wealth based on their own labor. However, that labor-based economy created a

---

5. Ashford, Robert, "Binary Economics: An Overview" (2010). Syracuse University College of Law - Faculty Scholarship. 15. https://surface.syr.edu/lawpub/15

6. Ibid.

standard of living more like a peasant compared to a middle-class worker in today's binary economy. In 1789, the average income in the North was $60-$80, which translates to a purchasing power of about $2,000 to $3,000 today.[7] This was a subsistence life compared to an average middle-class income of $80,000 today, and there was little access to health care or other things that greatly improve the standard of living today.

In the 19th century, technological advances and industrialization accelerated rapidly, driven by steel mills and railroads. The capital-to-labor ratio of production increased every year. Kelso believed the ratio would be reversed by the year 2000, with capital accounting for over 90 percent of production.[8]

The quality of life made possible by capitalism is enormous, even though the profits from capital income only directly benefit a small percentage of the people. Capitalism itself is not the problem, but the distribution of the ownership of and income from capital.

The wealth generated by capital compared to labor is so great that some people are adopting a reverse unitary economic theory, one based on capital instead of labor. The World Economic Forum (WEF) promotes a neo-mercantilist economic ideology, in which all value is derived from capital. Individual laborers are considered to be surplus population, unnecessary for advanced economies. Yuval Noah Harari, historian, futurist, and WEF adviser, said,

> We just don't need the vast majority of the population" in the early 21st century given modern technologies' rendering human labor economically and militarily "redundant.[9]

Harari spoke as if the "vast majority of the population" has no value except for their labor, and those who own the capital can live without them. Like the mercantilists who controlled their populations and

7. CPI Inflation Calculator. https://www.officialdata.org/us/inflation/1790.

8. Louis O. Kelso interview by Harold Channer. https://www.youtube.com/watch?v=lRPT3SFkndA.

9. Robert Kraychik. "WEF Adviser Yuval Harari: 'We Just Don't Need the Vast Majority of the Population' in Today's World, *Breibart,* August 10, 2022.

colonies to maximize their own wealth, Harari implies that people have no intrinsic value and those with wealth have no obligation to see them become economically autonomous. Depopulation and euthanasia become acceptable methods to avoid the burden of the wealthy minority to care for large numbers of people.

The increase in production by capital should not mean that human beings have no value. This goes against core Western beliefs as expressed in "the greatest sentence ever written in the Declaration of Independence:[10]

> We hold these truths to be self-evident, that all men are created equal, that they are endowed by their Creator with certain unalienable Rights, that among these are Life, Liberty, and the pursuit of Happiness.[11]

Integral economics accepts this statement. If an economy is capital-based, then everyone should be able to earn an income from capital. People are not redundant if their value is not solely derived from their labor value. An economy should enable all people to pursue happiness through the ownership of both their labor and their capital. Policies should seek wider ownership of capital, not the reduction of populations.

Ironically, Harari's statement is wrong in that large numbers of people are economically redundant. They are interdependent. Even if labor is not needed for production, the population is needed to purchase the goods produced by advanced technologies, or the economy will collapse and the rich will grow poor. The solution to capital income replacing labor income is for everyone to receive capital income. That is binary economics.

## F.A. Hayek and Three Spontaneous Orders

Frederich A. Hayek's discussion of spontaneous orders offers a strong corrective to Marxist materialism, economic reductionism, or mercantilism.

---

10. Walter Isaacson, *The Greatest Sentence Ever Written,* New York: Simon and Schuster, 2025.

11. Thomas Jefferson, et. al., The United States Declaration of Independence, second sentence. Following Jean-Jacques Burlamaqui, *The Principles of Natural and Politic Law,* orig. 1748, the founders considered property a natural right, but not an end in itself but in service of moral perfection.

Drawing on the work of Adam Smith, David Hume, Bernard Mandeville, Carl Menger, and Adam Ferguson, Hayek wrote of three "spontaneous natural orders" that arise in any human community—language, money, and law.[12] Hayek called these "the three paradigms of spontaneously occurring institutions." Together they generate an extended social order, a complex, self-organizing system far beyond any central manager's comprehension or control.

The evolution of human society is not rooted in one spontaneous order, but in all three. Integral economic theory, unlike ideologies that reduce society to wealth or power, recognizes that the family and community are the primary source of individual development, including economic autonomy. The government best serves as a referee that guarantees a fair economic playing field for all.

## G. W. F. Hegel and the Ethical Framework of Institutions

Mercantilists and selfish individuals strategically use institutions for their personal benefit, concentrating wealth and power for themselves. This is a form of theft from people, hidden by legal but unethical use of economic institutions. Modern political theory since Thomas Hobbes recognizes that this inevitably happens when a king or a minority group comes to control the state. Social contract theory and checks and balances on political power were developed in the U.S. Constitution. The focus has been on the state, but the temptation to co-opt power and wealth occurs in all institutions.

G. W. F. Hegel originated the science of studying social institutions as objective frameworks, as opposed to the subjective will of individuals. He developed this distinction in his three works: *Phenomenology of Spirit, Philosophy of Right*, and *Philosophy of History*.

Hegel elaborated on the distinction between individuals, institutions,

12. James U. Blanchard III and F. A. Hayek, "Exclusive Interview with F.A. Hayek," Cato Institute Policy Report, May-June 1984. https://www.cato.org/policy-report/may/june-1984/exclusive-interview-fa-hayek#

and God by systematically dividing *Geist* (spirit/mind/consciousness) into three main aspects: *subjektiver Geist* (Subjective Spirit), *objektiver Geist* (Objective Spirit), and absoluter Geist (Absolute Spirit).[13]

Individuals have a subjective consciousness rooted in their biological existence: brains, sense perception, and will to act. Historically, the internal moral/ethical life (*subjektiver geist*) has been the focus of religion and philosophy. Cultural traditions like Hammurabi's code, Greek, Roman, and Christian virtues, and Confucian and Buddhist philosophy explain values, norms, and habits that individuals practice to control their own actions. These traditions have taught about the subjective spirit.

However, the institutions that nourish these traditions are *objektiver Geist* (Objective Spirit). They embody formulated expressions in narratives that lie external to the individual subjects. Social institutions like religions and governments do not have subjective consciousness but embody an objective spirit based on their institutional purpose, rules, processes, and structures.

In *The Philosophy of History,* Hegel described human history as a dialectical development, or evolutionary dynamic, of the interrelation between *subjektiver Geist* and *objektiver Geist,* which aims at the embodiment of the *absoluter Geist* in the world. The *absoluter Geist,* which some call God, aims to create an institutional framework with an ethical order of rational freedom. Absolute Spirit reflects on, comprehends, and completes the developments of Objective Spirit. It lies alongside or beyond institutions like the state, art, religion, and philosophy.

Hegel saw the modern state of Prussia as the highest historical embodiment of the objective spirit. The constitutional monarchy actualizes freedom concretely through law, estates, and bureaucracy that protect the freedom of all. The Protestant Reformation was crucial in internalizing freedom in the individual conscience, allowing the secular state to become the dominant ethical power. Hegel sees this as a historical culmination in which the idea of freedom is actualized.

---

13. G.W.F. Hegel, addressed this tripartite structure of "spirit" (or consciousness) in three works translated to English: *Hegel's Phenomenology of Spirit, Hegel's Philosophy, of Right,* and *The Philosophy of History.*

Hegel is criticized as being too uncritical of the Prussian monarchy, the juncture where the objective spirit and the subjective spirit meet. The rational constitutional form requires the formal "I will" of individuals who will perfectly administer the state. Those people require a perfected subjective consciousness to carry out their tasks. His philosophy embodied a rational idealism that imagined a matured system in which freedom had been secured temporarily, but could later be lost to the likes of Hitler. The framework of freedom provided by the state required a subjective consciousness of individual moral agents to keep the machinery of the state running ethically.

Hegel also saw the structures of family, civil society, and state as the *objective* realization of freedom—*Sittlichkeit*—and insisted that individual moral agency is only fully intelligible within all these institutional forms. Most of his critics attacked his view of the state, but failed to see that family and other personal institutions were an integral part of Hegel's system.

Hayek's observations support the idea that the family and private property are necessary for the survival of the state, even though many ideologues and governments try to undermine them:

> The morals of property and the family were spread, and came to dominate a large part of the world, not because those who accepted them were able rationally to convince others that they were correct, and certainly not because they themselves liked them, but because those groups who by accident did accept them prospered and multiplied more than others.[14]

Integral theory uses Hegel's tripartite understanding of Spirit and considers him a foundational figure in the analysis of social institutions as having an objective spirit. However, Hegel may have been naive in equating the objective spirit of the state as "ethical." The Prussian state may have provided more freedom than preceding governments based on the arbitrary rule of power, but later bureaucratic states became unethical totalitarian regimes in which individuals had little or no freedom.

---

14. Frederick A. Hayek, "The Presumption of Reason," draft prepared for the 14th International Conference on the Unity of the Sciences, Houston, Texas, 1985. © 1986, International Cultural Foundation,

However, individual freedom is only one goal of social institutions; they can serve the development of individual moral agency, economic autonomy, provide a level playing field, and provide guardrails that curb harmful behavior.

The state only embodies one of three major aspects of spontaneous social life: the *law*. It can be an ethical framework that sets boundaries on the use of human freedom, but this is distinct from laws related to *cultural* and *economic* institutions that are also necessary for the attainment of a good life.

An integral consciousness understands how the social institutions in all three social spheres should function integrally and that the *objektiver Geis*t is only partly embodied in the State and partly embodied in other social institutions. The important conclusion is that Hegel's tripartite understanding of social consciousness lays a foundation for understanding the relationships among subjective individuals, objective institutions, and higher consciousness (or God).

This historical background helps to explain several theoretical aspects of an integral economy:

1. Free individuals with economic autonomy are the moral agents who are the essence and engines of society.
2. From 16th-century mercantilism onward, economic institutions have been used to centralize wealth. This must be reformed.
3. An integral economy is based on positive-sum relations that produce more than individuals laboring for themselves.
4. Productive value is binary—labor and capital.
5. There are three institutional spheres in society: culture, economy, and governance.
6. Institutions can be reformed to provide a more ethical framework for freedom, development, and wealth distribution.
7. The objective spirit of economic institutions should evolve from centralizing to decentralizing wealth.

# Chapter 2

## The Philosophical Framework

**Figure 1: Integral Society—A Head, a Body, and Two Wings**

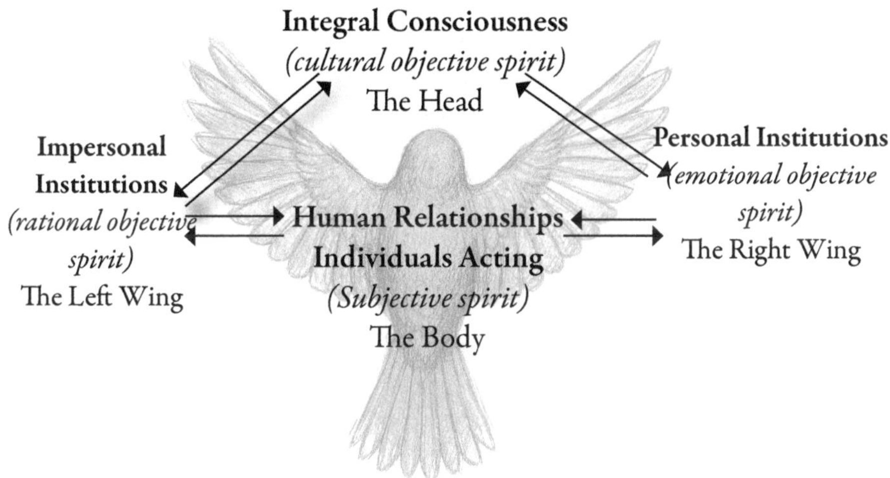


### Diagramming an Integral Society

**Figure 1** uses the image of a bird to convey the structure of an integral society. The bird is only an analogy to society, but it helps in reframing the terms left-wing and right-wing of society. In *Integral Society,* we used Ken Wilber's four quadrants and added a z-axis to diagram the evolutionary development of society.[1] Here, we use a bird to capture the relationships between individual moral agents, personal institutions, impersonal

1. Gordon L. Anderson, I*ntegral Society: Social Institutionas and Individual Sovereignty* (St. Paul, MN: Paragon House, 2023), pp. 161-163.

institutions, and cultural consciousness. The two wings and the head represent three aspects of objective consciousness that inform, develop, and provide guardrails on the subjective behavior of individual moral agents.

## Left and Right Wings

In common politics, we have right-wing and left-wing parties. The right wing promotes traditional values, personal responsibility, and individual freedom, with government often viewed as an intrusion that should be minimized. The left wing emphasizes state control, social justice, and restrictions on personal activity, with a tendency to micromanage individuals and replace personal institutions like family and community. In contemporary politics, these two wings struggle to control society, imposing their limited consciousness on individuals and the rest of society.

But society cannot fly on one wing. In an integral view, both wings are necessary, just like the left and right halves of the brain, one half based on sensory perception and emotion and the other on abstract rational thought. In an integral society, left and right are integrated in the head to ensure the balance so both wings can carry the body in flight.

## Personal and Impersonal Relationships

There are natural distinctions between personal and impersonal relations in what institutions on each wing can and cannot do. We constantly hear progressive politicians promising to make laws for impersonal institutions to provide personal care, but by nature they cannot. We also hear traditionalists saying social justice can be achieved solely through voluntary actions of moral agents. But moral agents are players with limited experience, not rational frameworks that govern the playing field.

These distinctions become very important for analyzing social institutions. For example, a personal banker can drive by a house and see how a borrower cares for the property he approves a mortgage. An impersonal subprime mortgage broker in a skyscraper in New York only knows the borrower's credit score and the application paperwork that appears on his desk, with no confidence that they are accurate without personal experience.

**Figure 2: Integral Society—Levels**

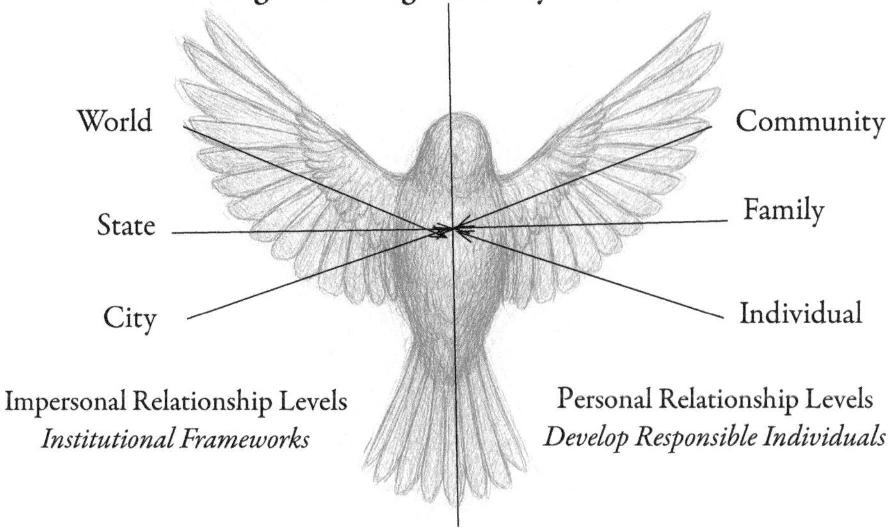


**Figure 2** shows different levels of society. It is important to understand the difference between *personal* and *impersonal* levels of society.

## Personal Levels

On a personal level, individuals interact through face-to-face relationships. This creates immediate sense perceptions integrated in individual brains. We associate these relationships with subjectivity—the right wing and even the right brain—because they involve emotion. At the personal level, individual needs are better addressed. For example, in the family, the parents can provide direct care for children. They know immediately if they are cold, hungry, sick, or injured and can respond accordingly. A member of a community who sees another drowning can jump in the water and rescue them. Impersonal institutions do not know these things.

## Impersonal Levels

Relations on impersonal levels are more abstract and indirect. They involve rational processes and rules that apply to everyone. Impersonal institutions often get information from filled-out forms, or meeting an agent you don't know at a counter who strictly follows institutional rules.

Impersonal institutions, like the state, are rational, like the left brain, and can accordingly be called the left wing. They are analytically constructed to perform functions based on rules. Impersonal institutions cannot directly care for or love individuals. An impersonal institution doesn't know if a child is bleeding or if the snow in someone's driveway has been removed. But an impersonal hospital bureaucracy can provide a doctor for a bleeding child that a parent brings in. A state can plow the main road that connects to everyone's driveway.

The tendency to centralize knowledge, power, or wealth and the temptation to use impersonal institutions to control personal interactions causes social dysfunction. Decentralization is necessary for personal, humane relationships and individual happiness. Society needs to understand and balance the roles of impersonal and personal life. When the extreme left asks the impersonal state to eliminate the family, dysfunction occurs. When a libertarian argues to get rid of the state, dysfunction occurs. Individuals, personal institutions, and impersonal institutions all have their place in an integral society.

## The Body

The diagram in **Figure 1** *(above)* portrays the body of society as the world of human relationships. Imagine the body as the playing field, with players running across it, trained by the coaches on the right wing and the impersonal institutions on the left wing acting as referees and enforcing the penalties for violating rules. Personal institutions like family and community create the human capital[2] of the individuals. Economic institutions like shareholder-owned corporations facilitate a return on the individual's labor and capital.[3] The bird flies well when the game is not rigged. Captured institutions serve their leaders rather than their function in creating ethical and productive players and a level playing field.

2. *Merriam-Webster Dictionary:* The skills, knowledge, and qualifications of a person, group, or workforce considered as economic assets

3. An individual's human capital value serves both their labor value and capital production value.

The rules for both the institutions and the individuals should come from the objective social consciousness in the head, which represents the highest knowledge civilization has developed.

In the body of society, all kinds of relations take place. There are three major social spheres that exist at many levels, from the individual to the global. The institutional framework on the left wing is not only the state, which Hegel emphasized, but also rational and impersonal rules of culture and economy integrally related to other levels of social governance

Social Spheres

**Figure 3: Integral Society—Spheres**

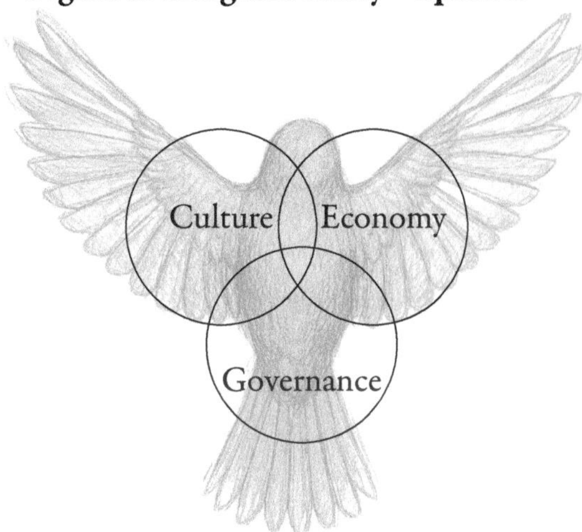


**Figure 3** shows three spheres that are independent but overlap. They represent Hayek's three spontaneous orders that arise in all societies: communication, economic exchange, and law. These three spheres have different functions, like the organs of the human body. A liver cannot house consciousness; that is the role of the brain. A government cannot produce goods; that is the role of a corporation. But both are required for the whole complex social system to operate.

Social spheres involve the personal and impersonal levels of society. In economics, microeconomics generally refers to the personal levels and macroeconomics to the impersonal institutional frameworks. The same is true in other spheres.

Ideologies constantly confuse the different functions of social wings, spheres, and levels with reductionist arguments. Serious social dysfunction arises when the state is asked to do things economic or cultural institutions naturally do. Dysfunction also occurs when an impersonal state is asked to do something only a personal institution can do.

Political parties and omnibus legislation are used by special interests to create laws that ignore such distinctions and cause harm to everyone who has to subsidize that interest. Recent fraudulent distribution of federal funds by states has shown how easy it is for unscrupulous people to lie on forms and steal money from impersonal institutions that don't have adequate methods of verification of the information on the forms. This requires an integral consciousness.

## The Head

The head is the repository of objective social consciousness. An integral objective consciousness is the minimum level of consciousness for a sustainable, functional society. We should seek to develop a higher consciousness, aiming at what Hegel called the absolute, or God consciousness, but we should not be as pretentious as Hegel to believe it can be embodied in the state, or in human consciousness.

Like the owl of Minerva spreading its wings at dusk, subjective individuals should contemplate activities that have taken place, seeking to improve the objective consciousness in the head. The knowledge in the head should be encyclopedic, encompassing everything known. Unfortunately, dogmatic, ideological, and absolutist thinking attempts to control the head, filtering out information needed for an integral society.

### Development of the Objective Spirit in the Head

The conflicts between right-wing and left-wing thought are rooted in dogmatic, ideological, and absolutist consciousness. The dogmatic form of absolutism on the right is called reactionary and the absolutist form on the left revolutionary. Both forms of absolutism reflect naive, immature, and pre-integral consciousness. Tribalism and censorship are products of this type of thinking.

Sociologist Ernst Troeltsch wrote about the importance of transforming naive forms of absoluteness into genuine wisdom, in which comparisons are made and only proven errors in received worldviews are rejected. Unfalsified views were carried forward in tradition, with the assumption that they may serve some non-rational evolutionary purpose.[4]

Philosopher Karl Popper similarly argued that it is not scientific to reject received truth simply because it was not proved by science; rather, science can only reject received knowledge when it is proven false: falsified.[5] This is an important concept for an "open society" in which no "ism" closes minds. Students should be taught not to naively reject inherited ideas, or naively accept doctrines promoted by great leaders.

Popper knew that the truth can be very uncomfortable for people. He fled Austria after the Nazi takeover in 1938 because he was Jewish. In his preface to *The Open Society and Its Enemies,* he wrote:

> If in this book harsh words are spoken about some of the greatest among the intellectual leaders of mankind, my motive is not, I hope, to belittle them. It springs rather from my conviction that, if our civilization is to survive, we must break with the habit of deference to great men.[6]

In T*he Structure of Scientific Revolutions,* Thomas Kuhn described the difficulty of scientific disciplines accepting new theories. Science, like religion, is based on a measure of faith in received theories that may be taken by practitioners as absolute. New theories and paradigms are often initially rejected by the guardians of the scientific community, who rose

---

4. 4. Ernst Troeltsch, *The Absoluteness of Christianity and the History of Religions* (Richmond, VA: John Knox, 1971). See. Chapter 6, Two Types of Absoluteness, pp. 131-163.

5. Karl Popper, *The Logic of Scientific Discovery,* First published in German in 1935 and in English in 1959,

6. Karl Popper, *The Open Society and Its Enemies,* (1945).

to their positions espousing now-obsolete ideas. Eventually, better theories should win out as they gain wider acceptance, and the more stubborn scientists finally back down:

> An apparently arbitrary element, compounded of personal and historical accident, is always a formative ingredient of the beliefs espoused by a given scientific community at a given time....[7]

In *Against Method,* Paul Feyerabend explained that the received traditions might first look like myths, but often contain deeper truths not seen on the surface, or as products of reason:

> Today we realize that rationalism, being bound to science, cannot give us any assistance in the issue between science and myth, and we must also know, from inquiries of an entirely different kind, the myths are vastly better than rationalists have dared to admit. Thus, we are now forced to raise the question of the excellence of science. An examination then reveals that science and myth overlap in many ways, that the differences we think we perceive are often local phenomena which may turn into similarities elsewhere and that fundamental discrepancies are the results of different aims rather than different methods trying to reach one and the same "rational" end (such as, for example, "progress," or increase of content, or "growth").[8]

Friedrich Hayek concludes that reason and the moral order have evolved along two separate paths. Moral evolution and rational evolution were two different types of valid evolution of human knowledge, and one could not legitimately reject the other:

> Our morality, whose explanation and justification has seemed so unsatisfactory, is as much the result of an evolutionary selection process as is our reason, which, however stems from a separate development, so that one should never suppose that our reason is in the highest critical

7. Thomas S. Kuhn, *The Structure of Scientific Revolutions* (Chicago: University of Chicago Press, 1962), 4.

8. Paul Feyerabend, *Against Method: Outline of an Anarchistic Theory of Knowledge* (London: New Left Books, 1975), 295.

position and that only those moral rules are valid which our reason endorses. Certain moral rules which are not obvious to our reason nonetheless are the conditions for mankind being able to reach its current numbers.[9]

These two paths, the moral and rational, represent the left and right sides of the brain in individuals, and of objective consciousness of the left- and right-wing social institutions in society.

## Transcend and Include

Integral thinkers refer to this evolutionary process of thought as "transcend and include."[10] This means that people transcend their previous knowledge and consciousness by including new information and discarding information that may be falsified.

**Figure 4. Transcend and Include**

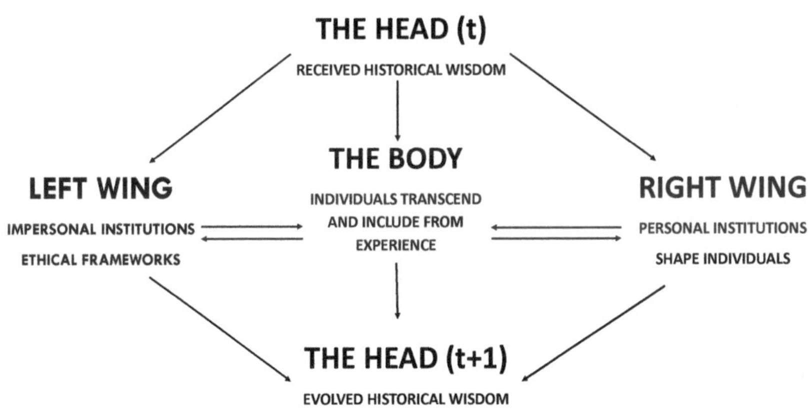


**Figure 4** illustrates this dynamic in our integral institutional framework, where both right- and left-wing institutions are informed by the head as they shape and serve individuals acting in society, who will advance the

9. Frederich Hayek, "The Presumption of Reason," http://blog.ganderson.us/2011/12/the-presumption-of-reason/.

10. Allan Combs, "Transcend and Include: Ken Wilber's Contribution to Transpersonal Psychology," in *The Wiley-Blackwell Handbook of Transpersonal Psychology* (John Wiley & Sons, 2015), pp.166-186.

objective collective consciousness of society. Over time, consciousness advances through levels or stages.

### Stages of Consciousness

**Figure 5. Stages of Cultural Consciousness**

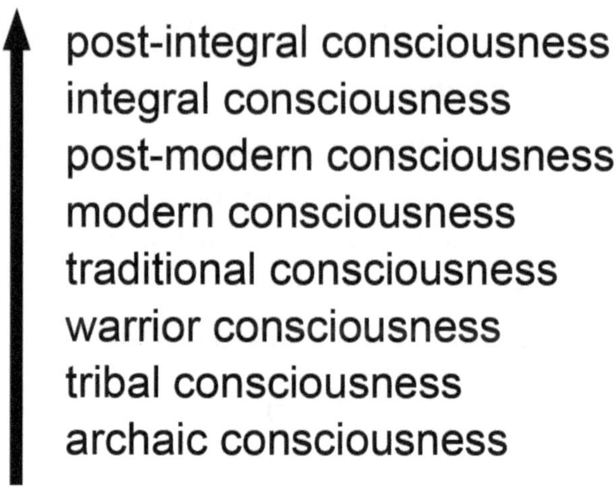


**Figure 5** portrays the evolution of levels of consciousness from least to highest evolved (from bottom up). Steve McIntosh provides detailed descriptions of the characteristics of these stages in *Integral Consciousness and the Future of Evolution.*[11]

Archaic consciousness would have no social consciousness except for animal instincts. Tribal consciousness mirrors the objective consciousness of an immediate social group. Warrior consciousness develops from competition with other tribes over resources and stresses conquest and plunder at the cost of one's life if necessary. Traditional consciousness involves the agrarian basis of production, diversified skills, and moral values promoted by cultural narratives and the leaders of society. Modern consciousness includes reason, science, and technological developments

11. Steve McIntosh, *Integral Consciousness and the Future of Evolution* (St. Paul, MN: Paragon House, 2007), pp. 34-84.

that can improve life, but ethnic groups and states clash over land and resources. Post-modern consciousness recognizes pluralism and seeks ways that people of different religious, ethnic, racial, and political differences can live together. Integral consciousness has developed sufficiently to produce productive, responsible individuals and ethical institutional frameworks that support a functional society. Post-integral consciousness pursues beauty, truth, goodness, and happiness beyond what is necessary for social functionality.

Paul Smith's book *Integral Christianity,*[12] provides an excellent historical review of the Christian churches and culture, explaining the various levels of objective consciousness manifest in the evolutionary forms of Christian culture. Smith describes manifestations of tribal church, warrior church, modern church, and postmodern church, calling the church to become integral. This type of analysis can be applied to any social institution. This book focuses on an integral economy.

## Integral Economic Consciousness

An integral economy requires an integral economic consciousness. Unfortunately, cultural economic consciousness has not reached stages as high as either political or economic consciousness. Most economic discussions reflect traditional and modern consciousness. Of course, there are religious fanatics and political movements that still fight tooth and nail with warrior consciousness. However, most people believe in religious and political pluralism and impersonal institutions that allow membership to people of all backgrounds.

Today's capitalist, socialist, and communist economies are all centrally controlled. Most people still argue about which of these centrally controlled systems is better and are not thinking about alternative decentralized economic systems. The people in power want to keep it that way.

Bitcoin and some other cryptocurrencies are attempts to break free of the stranglehold that states and central banks have over money, thus

12. Paul R. iSmith, *Integral Christianity: There Spirit's Call to Evolve,* Paragon House, 2011.

pushing economic consciousness towards pluralism. However, the desire to be freed from central economic control is still two stages below integral economic consciousness. The banking system will need to be decentralized in an integral economy, with central banks transformed from players into referees.

Post-modern economic consciousness is better found in capitalist corporations owned by many individuals who purchase shares on an open market, regardless of the religious, ethnic, or class background. This reflects pluralism, although modern states still interfere with the ethical distribution of profits with laws and tax strategies that tend to concentrate profits in the hands of interlopers rather than enabling the maximum distribution of profits to the shareholders who are the rightful owners.

Corporations can play a major role in an integral economy without significant changes in the way they are chartered. However, tax policies and laws related to the distribution of profits should change so that profits are distributed widely to public shareholders. This can enable everyone to generate an income stream from capital they invest in corporate shares.

Individual and family businesses or partnerships are personal economic institutions that are primarily based on labor, as the trades and shops in the 18th century. However, as they grow large, become capital intensive, and impersonal, this is no longer the case. Therefore, we suggest that when they become impersonal economic companies, they should be publicly traded.

Impersonal institutions should act as referees and serve everyone and not certain individuals exclusively. Most corporations already go public before they are valued at $10 billion. We propose that this becomes a rule. This dovetails with binary economic theory that holds everyone should be able to earn an income from both labor and capital.

Decentralization of wealth will be perceived as a threat to establishment centralizers, as their zero-sum economics involves some form of theft. They expect a new system to take from them. This is not necessary. A new integral economic system can be born by reforming the old system to have wider and more just capital income distribution going forward.

This is the integral concept of transcend and include in the evolution of capitalism. People can keep the wealth they have, but lose future unethical acquisition of new wealth through centralized control of financial institutions, or fiat money printing.

## Positive-Sum Production

Zero-sum economics is based on foraging and theft rather than production and voluntary exchange. Foraging is an economic activity based on the survival instinct. Hunter-gatherer society is a form of foraging, living off of things they did not produce. This is zero-sum economics because, without human cultivation, nature produces a limited supply of food. Foraging is a form of dependency, not economic autonomy.

Warrior consciousness is rooted in foraging and theft. Civilization begins with agriculture, the human production of food. Human beings are creators who can work with nature to produce enough for themselves and have a surplus to trade from their own land. Agriculture with significant surpluses frees people to produce and trade other things, to have time for recreation, and to live without needing to fight others. This is positive-sum production.

Adam Smith's theory of markets and trade is based on positive-sum production. He opposed the mercantilists, who developed a colonial foraging superstructure that overlaid agricultural civilization. They acquired gold, silver, land, and other things that made them wealthy. Mercantilism allowed natives and peasants enough food to survive, but the other wealth generated was centralized. The Spanish Empire was built on plunder from its colonies.

Positive-sum production benefits every individual producer. There is no need to kill others if you are a producer and can trade. You prefer more people making different things because it increases your own standard of living. Smith's argument was persuasive in a labor-based economy. But this principle has not been adequately developed for a binary economy. The capitalist economic system must be reformed so it can become a positive-sum asset for everyone.

## Economic Institutions are Tools

Social institutions make it possible for people to freely pursue happiness without being subjected to the arbitrary rule of people in positions of power. Capitalist economic institutions, even in their unethical forms with unfair distribution of capital income, have greatly increased the standard of living for most people. They have made it possible for the average working person to have about $75,000 in purchasing power, compared to $2,000 or $3,000 in today's money in 1789.

The existence of capitalist institutions is not the problem; it is the way people understand them, how they are owned, how they are regulated, and how they are managed. They have enabled life to become so much better for people that they take them for granted. Just as Hegel made the mistake of equating the Prussian state with the absolute incarnate, many people expect social institutions to be their savior and provider. People look to institutions, either right-wing or left-wing institutions, as competing gods that will take responsibility for us, but they cannot.

Institutions are objective tools created to help raise productive and responsible individuals, streamline work, and provide a level playing field for people to pursue happiness. When people think impersonal institutions are subjective saviors, rather than objective frameworks, unscrupulous people will hijack them with false promises of salvation. They should foster individual autonomy, but get weaponized to centralize power and wealth. In an integral economy, economic wealth should be maximally decentralized, with institutions as tools designed for that purpose.

The Supreme Court caused great confusion on this matter with the decision that corporations are "persons."[13] The term "persons" is a legal fiction. The Court ruled that the Southern Pacific Railroad had legal protection from being arbitrarily taxed by Santa Clara County. It drew on the 14th Amendment, designed as an anti-slavery measure, saying that states must treat all persons equally. Institutions, even though they are tools, need protection from abuse, but calling corporations "persons" has

13. *Santa Clara County v. Southern Pacific Railroad Company,* decided on May 10, 1886 [118 U.S. 394 (1886)].

led people to treat them as subjective individuals. This enables people to use them, and even treat them in law, as subjective individuals with enormously more power and wealth, creating social injustice. For example, allowing corporations, NGOs, or other institutions to lobby government officials effectively turns citizens into their tools. Institutions as "persons" pay political parties to provide them benefits at the expense of individual taxpayers.

Like other tools, political and economic institutions can assist individuals in pursuing their goals. They can be used for good or bad purposes, enabling a positive-sum economic expansion where everyone gains, or negative-sum vehicles of wealth extraction for institutional leaders.

## Leadership Abuse

Economic institutions get hijacked by elites exercising bad moral agency. The right wing emphasizes better personal institutions that create more ethical individuals. The left wing emphasizes restructuring institutions. Both are correct; better individuals and better institutions should always be the goal. But making institutions better means making them more ethical tools, not giving these tools more power over individuals.

Even highly virtuous people are very tempted by positions in control of money and power. The misuse of institutional power or public money is an insidious form of theft because it is difficult to detect. Individuals are not literally mugged, and most people assume an institution will act honestly. However, most institutions can be reformed to become more ethical frameworks that are more difficult for leaders to abuse.

## Ideological and Political Capture

Ideological capture redirects resources to ideological goals, shifting funds meant to serve individuals' pursuit of happiness to institutions that were established to support ideological institutions or political parties.

Most communist or socialist ideologues complain about the unfair distribution of wealth by capitalists. They argue that the state should take over ownership of industries or tax them heavily and redistribute the profits from production by force. Such arguments, often based on envy and resentment, appeal to young or oppressed people who have not experienced economic autonomy or learned why such theories harm society. Communists always use political parties and their own institutions to centralize control of wealth and distribute it as the leaders saw fit. This is zero-sum economics that destroys the individual incentive to invent and produce, except on a black market.

In the United States, political parties are lobbied by ideological donors who have amassed more political money than individual citizens could hope to raise. NGOs legally act as "persons" competing against corporations also acting as "persons." Democrats tend to support zero-sum policies that redistribute wealth for special interests and promote state structures that undermine the personal institutions of family and community. Republicans tend to promote lower taxes, smaller government, and less corporate regulation. In either case, political parties become vehicles for legislation that favors institutional interests rather than the interests of individual citizens.

## Approaching An Integral Economy

The 2008 economic collapse and bailout for institutions "too big to fail" signaled the end of parties serving special interests as usual. Donald Trump, a former Democrat, ran as a Republican on a populist pro-working-class ticket in 2016, causing a backlash from established party interests on both sides. Party and institutional control of governments around the world has led to a revival of populism worldwide.

Reforming economic institutions requires changes in the laws that prevent their capture and remove their influence on government. The objective consciousness in the head must become integral. Looking at today's politics, this might seem an impossible task. However, as Ken Wilber suggests, a small percentage of leading-edge thinkers, perhaps 10 percent of the population, can create a "tipping point" to advance the next stage of social evolution. In his discussion of pluralistic consciousness, he suggests that the U.S. moved from about 2–3 percent pluralist in 1959 to 10 percent during the 1960s, fueling cultural movements for civil rights, feminism, and environmentalism.

Today, this pluralistic consciousness may be at 23–25 percent. However, when the 1960s elites became embedded in politics, they sought to dominate institutions, succumbing to the temptation to power and spurring the search for a more integral consciousness.[14] Today, the leading edge of integral consciousness may be approaching 7-9 percent. These are people who have moved from postmodern consciousness to integral.[15] We might be closing in on a 10 percent tipping point that can bring reforms that can make society integral.

In the following chapters, we will discuss reforms guided by our integral framework that led to an integral economy. This might be as unsettling to the economic establishment as Luther's 95 theses were to the Catholic Church. It might also help us reach that needed tipping point.

---

14. Ken Wilber, *Trump and a Post-Truth World,* (Boulder CO: Shambala, 2017), pp. 113-131.

15. Markus Plesner Dalin's Post, *Integral Global* facebook group. https://www.facebook.com/groups/164677653606701/posts/7630629933678065/

# Part 2

## Money and Banking

# Chapter 3

## Wealth and Money

Individual ownership of wealth—property, assets, capital, and one's own labor—is a fundamental right in an integral society. In the previous chapters, we referred to the importance of ownership in the thought of Aristotle, Adam Smith, and F. A. Hayek. The cumulative effect of individuals engaged in economic relationships to pursue happiness is the driving force of the economy. People need free, fair, and just access to economic opportunity and wealth. They also need personal development and skills to achieve economic autonomy and manage wealth responsibly in a free economic system.

### Wealth Metrics

People are currently classified economically by their annual income. In the U.S., "middle-class" is considered to be between $56,600 and $169,800 for a three-person household, depending on where one lives.[1] But money is only one aspect of wealth; the truest standard of wealth would be economic independence based on assets. Someone who owns a house and land, grows their own food, and produces their own electricity does not require a large annual income to live a secure, economically autonomous life. On the other hand, someone who receives a larger income but is strapped by debt, rent, car payments, and school loans is

1. Richard Fry, *Pew Research,* Sept. 18, 2024. https://www.pewresearch.org/short-reads/2024/09/16/are-you-in-the-american-middle-class/

not economically autonomous and is often stressed and overworked. A farmer who earns $10,000 per year might have more economic autonomy than a city dweller earning $100,000 per year. Further, for the middle class, more than 90 percent of income comes from wage labor and employer benefits, and less than 10 percent from capital investments. Middle- and lower-income people are classified by their wage labor value.

Most of the wealth generated by capital remains concentrated in the upper classes. Income based on capital is taxed at a lower rate than wage income, structurally contributing to wealth concentration. Fair wealth distribution laws will need to treat income from capital and labor equally.

Individual economic autonomy is not well correlated with annual income. Net worth is a better indicator of autonomy. Someone with a high annual income may appear wealthy, but if their future is controlled by others like landlords and bankers, they are not economically autonomous. A better metric of economic autonomy is net worth, or some combination of net worth and annual income.

Next is the problem of using Gross Domestic Product (GDP) as a metric to measure economic development. GDP represents the total production of a state's economy, but it is not a good measure of the economic well-being of the people. All of the growth in GDP might go to the top 1 percent, with most people gaining little or moving backward in terms of economic autonomy. A better indicator of the economic health of the society is the median (not average) net worth of individuals. Median wealth is a distributive measurement. It is the value that describes the line at which half the population is above, and half is below. If median wealth is rising, we are looking at economic improvement for the majority of people, not just the wealthy.

As we evaluate economic institutions from an integral perspective, we will consider median ownership of wealth, rather than national GDP or annual paychecks. Economic institutions should provide a framework that facilitates the largest possible percentage of autonomous individual moral agents on the economic playing field. The economic system should naturally distribute wealth rather than concentrate or redistribute it. These metrics help us to understand wealth distribution.

## Money

Money is a vehicle for the exchange of wealth; it represents wealth but may not be a physical asset like gold or silver. A dollar bill or an electronic ledger transaction has no *intrinsic value* but has an *exchange value* determined by the physical assets it can purchase.

## Money as a Spontaneous Order

Money is to an economy as food is to a body. It can come in different forms—from barter to an electronic transaction—but is as necessary for economic institutions to operate. F. A. Hayek explained that the appearance of money is one of three core *spontaneous* orders in society. Spontaneous orders are social institutions that arise as the unintended but natural result of individuals pursuing their own interests.

Money emerges to address practical needs of trade. Hayek expanded on Carl Menger's 1892 essay "On the Origin of Money." The first step is barter; next, people seek inventive ways to make trading easier, agreeing on commodities like grain or precious metals that have a reliable market value. This is money. No one invented it, but it was the unintended byproduct of thousands or millions of economic trade relations. Hayek saw state control of money as a *constructed* order that was unable to facilitate trade as well as natural money spontaneously arising from individuals exchanging goods and services.

The distinction between spontaneous order and constructed order can be compared to the difference between individuals as subjective agents and institutions as objective frameworks. The objective framework is constructed and becomes ethical when it serves the individual relationships on the economic playing field.

## Gold-Based Money

Grain, shells, gold, and other physical objects were used as money in earlier societies. More recently, paper notes became widely used. Initially, paper notes were redeemable in gold or silver.

In the 19th century, the U.S. was on a gold standard, and there were many economic booms and busts, expansions and contractions. This is because individuals' desire to produce and expand the economy did not match the expansion of gold in the economy. When money is backed by gold and the economy expands, the value of gold increases following the principle of supply and demand. When the price of gold increased, further economic development was inhibited. Governments tried to fix this problem by setting the price of gold at a fixed rate, but as the true market value of gold rose compared to the government-set price, the government ran out of gold to back the notes.

The gold standard does not lead to a stable money system that provides reliable access to money or loans for individuals. A good money supply should expand and contract at the same rate individuals engage in production, trade, and other economic activities. It should serve the spontaneous order as individuals produce and exchange other goods and services.

After the bank panic of 1907, the Federal Reserve was promoted as a solution to economic instability. The idea was that the Federal Reserve could provide a more elastic currency and be a lender of last resort. However, it was centrally created and still based on a gold standard. The value of gold had been artificially set at $20.67 per ounce by the Gold Standard Act of 1900. The Fed was supposed to hold enough reserves to cushion banks in the event there was a run on gold. It was a "constructivist" solution that failed to match economic development in the spontaneous order in the long run. It also introduced "moral hazard" because banks felt they could take more risk with that cushion.

At the end of the 1920s, bank failures accelerated runs on the banks, causing a worse economic collapse than before the Federal Reserve was created. The first response by Franklin Roosevelt was to shore up the Federal Reserve with the Emergency Banking Act (March 5, 1933) and asked all individuals to turn in their gold. They were given three weeks and paid $20.67 per ounce. The Banking Act of 1933 (Glass-Steagall Act of June 16, 1933) separated commercial banking and investment banking and created the FDIC to guarantee individuals' deposits in case of bank failure. Then, the Gold Reserve Act (January 30, 1934) raised the price of gold to $35 per ounce. This boosted the government's balance sheet, but devalued the dollar 41 percent, causing people effectively to pay a one-time 41 percent tax on their money, transferring their wealth to the government. Roosevelt had saved banks—economic institutions—at the expense of individual citizens, many of whom lost jobs, economic autonomy, and subsisted throughout the 1930s.

The gold standard was a reason the depression was prolonged. It had been adjusted, but recovery was inhibited because the economy was related to a fixed amount of gold. This created a deflationary bias. Central banks defended gold reserves by raising interest rates and contracting money supplies.

The U.S. did not recover until after World War II. The official Keynesian view is that World War II ended the recession by ramping up war industries and "employing" 12 million soldiers. Women became workers in war production plants. The employment rate dropped from 17 percent in 1939 to 1.9 percent in 1945. GDP grew dramatically. The war was funded largely through borrowing. The national debt increased five times, from about $49 billion in 1941 to nearly $260 billion in 1945.

This does not fit an integral view of economic development, which uses median individual wealth as an indicator. The GDP figures did not represent the production of new wealth for citizens, but products consumed by war. Heavy-handed wage and price controls caused shortages and deprived the market economy of the ability to function spontaneously. Americans were strapped with the burden of the war debt. The WWII war economy resembled the growth of GDP in the post-war Soviet Union, where GDP soared while the standard of living did not.

The Austrian school of economists argues that the wartime recovery was a facade and just another aberration in the economy due to central government meddling. Our median wealth metrics would agree. The real recovery came after WWII when wartime economic restrictions were lifted and returning soldiers and wartime women workers were highly incentivized to start families and build personal wealth.

## Fiat Paper Money

In 1971, Richard Nixon unilaterally suspended the gold standard, causing another economic shock. This ended the system that pegged the dollar to gold. The move was driven by rising U.S. inflation, a growing balance-of-payments deficit, and heavy pressure on U.S. gold reserves from foreigners redeeming dollars for gold at a bargain price.

The dollar became a pure fiat currency, backed by government decree and trust rather than gold. The world moved to floating exchange rates. Overnight, the dollar decreased 25 percent compared to the German Mark. This began a period called "stagflation," high inflation combined with slow growth. In December 1980, under President Jimmy Carter, the prime interest rate hit 21.5 percent.

This was followed by an artificial recovery under Reagan with "supply-side economics" and "trickle-down" economic theories. This increased mergers, acquisitions, holding companies, and other forms of economic consolidation by financial institutions that leveraged existing wealth and offshored a substantial amount of manufacturing. The working class lost jobs while financial industries boomed. Cash was freed up for financial institutions to make capital investments in new production overseas, but the profits were largely realized on Wall Street.

The (ethical) Glass-Steagall Act of 1933, designed to separate banking and business speculation, was repealed in November 1999, allowing for the Citibank-Travelers Insurance merger. This led to (unethical) corporate raiding and scandals like Enron and WorldCom quickly followed. Corporate pension funds were sometimes dissolved by the raiders, depriving retirees of their promised benefits. This activity created Wall Street tycoons but not Main Street wealth. The financial system became propped up by speculation and trading of worthless loans as securities, leading to another economic collapse.

In 2010, 40-45 of the largest banks, those with over $50 billion in assets, were declared "too big to fail," and bailed out by federal loans. In 2018, this number was raised to $250 billion, halving the number of banks "too big to fail" in the highly centralized economy.

Neither the creation of the Federal Reserve nor the shift to fiat paper money solved the problems of economic instability. More elasticity was realized, but centralized control of money under either the government or the financial institutions caused several new problems: "counterfeiting," excessive borrowing, hidden taxes through inflation, and excessive institutional risk-taking.

The precariousness of this highly centralized fiat-money-based economy is alarming. Reforms are needed but have not been made. Senator Ron Paul ran on a platform to "End the Fed,"[2] audit Fort Knox, and return to the gold standard. Former Federal Reserve Chairman Paul Volcker pressed to reinstate the Glass-Steagall Act, returning to a more ethical banking system. Both these approaches proposed economic frameworks that had previously failed to enable stable economic expansion, based on the spontaneous needs of individuals desiring to produce and exchange.

## Ledger-Based Money

In this book, we propose banking reforms that align the money system with the spontaneous economic order rather than a gold standard or central bank control. The top-down system of money control should be replaced with a bottom-up system that ties the money supply to the production of new economic assets by individuals pursuing economic autonomy. The central bank should be changed from a player to a referee.

This proposal is not completely new. The Dutch Florin is an example of the utility of ledger currency. It was trusted and became the reserve currency of Europe for over 200 years. In 1609, the Bank of Amsterdam was created as an exchange bank. Coins and notes from all kinds of issuers flooded the market, and merchants had little idea of what they were worth. They needed a bank that graded the value of the different currencies and could exchange them for a reliable value.

The Bank of Amsterdam accepted the various coins for its reserve, and issued bank deposit books denominated in an accounting unit called

2. Ron Paul, *End the Feed,* Grand Central Publishing, 2010.

the florin. The florin was ledger currency that represented a fixed value and standard in relation to all the currencies being exchanged. Some people have referred to the florin as the world's first stablecoin.[3]

The name florin came from the city of Florence, where the highest-grade coins had previously been produced. However, no notes or coins called florins circulated. Rather, the amounts on an individual's deposit book were listed as florins. Withdrawals and deposits could be made in different currencies, but they would be converted to florins on the journal entry.

The Bank of Amsterdam was chartered by the City Council to act as a monetary exchange referee. It initially performed that single economic function. It was a spontaneous institution that arose to serve individuals' need for reliable money exchange. As the Bank of Amsterdam grew, it added more functions, emerging as the first central bank:

> By the end of the seventeenth century, the Bank of Amsterdam was performing three functions that are routinely carried out by central banks today: operating a large-value payment system, creating a form of money not directly redeemable for coin, and managing the value of this money through open market operations.[4]

Notes written redeemable as florins at the Bank of Amsterdam became more widely used than other notes or coins. They were not physical assets like gold coins, but they could be reliably exchanged for them. They replaced the need to carry around heavy amounts of gold for large transactions. Due to its tie to this ledger currency, the Dutch guilder became the reserve currency for Europe in the 17th and 18th centuries.[5]

---

3. Jon Frost, Hyun Song Shin and Peter Wierts, "An early stablecoin? The Bank of Amsterdam and the governance of money." BIS Working Papers, No 902, November 2020.

4. Stephen Quinn and William Roberds, "An Economic Explanation of the Early Bank of Amsterdam, Debasement, Bills of Exchange, and the Emergence of the First Central Bank," Federal Reserve Bank of Atlanta, Working Paper 2006-13. September 2006. https://www.atlantafed.org/research/publications/wp/2006/13.

5. tephen Quinn and William Roberds, "Death of a Reserve Currency," *International Journal of Central Banking,* December 2016, pp. 63-103.

The Bank of Amsterdam eventually succumbed to temptation and violated its core rule against lending money. First, it began to allow depositors to overdraw their accounts. Later, it secretly lent to the Dutch East India Company. The company ran up a massive debt that could not be repaid in 1779. Depositors began to lose trust in the bank, and a run on the bank made it "technically insolvent."[6] Another institution (the Dutch East India Company) had hijacked the bank's purpose, leading to failure.

The lesson provided by the Bank of Amsterdam is that it worked well as a central exchange bank that served as a money referee for individuals and was forbidden to act as a player. It accomplished what no central bank has done since: act strictly as a referee. Stephen Quinn and William Roberds argue that the Bank of Amsterdam avoided three problematic functions of modern central banks:

> Ironically, the Bank of Amsterdam may be best remembered for what it did not do, i.e., take on what are now viewed as the definitive central-bank functions of circulating note issue, operation of a discount window, and the purchase of government securities.[7]

In the following chapter on banking, we propose a central ledger system, functioning as a referee, more like the Bank of Amsterdam than a modern central bank. However, the Bank of Amsterdam did not have a mechanism to address the problem of a flexible money supply that matched spontaneous economic expansion. This requires fractional-reserve lending. However, we propose that lending and expansion remain with corresponding banks that are institutional players, separated from the central bank ledger that acts strictly as a referee.

---

6. This was not a complete insolvency, but a policy insolvency, because it carried more debt than reserves.

7. Stephen Quinn and William Roberds, "An Economic Explanation... .," *op. cit.*

# Chapter 4

## *An Integral Banking System*

An integral banking system is an integration of banking institutions that serve the needs of all individuals in the society. It allows access to everyone on an equal basis, and the system is designed to decentralize the distribution of wealth. The banks will use money that is integral, reflecting the spontaneous day-to-day activities of trading and producing by all economic players and refereed, not directed, centrally.

Chapter 3, on money, concludes with a discussion of the ledger system developed by the Bank of Amsterdam. This bank was organically related to the spontaneous activities of merchants and traders. As an exchange bank, it held precious metal deposits and maintained ledger currency accounts for exchange. This facilitated trading, but did not create new money for future economic production. An integral banking system must do both. It must facilitate the organic creation of new money to expand the economy as people need loans to build homes, and create productive industries that will generate a future return.

An integral banking system can be decentralized, with no central banks acting as players or holding reserves, and no big banks too big to fail. Money can be tied to the assets created and owned by all individuals in the society. The decentralized control of wealth will lead to a larger middle class. To avoid economic shock, there can be a gradual transition from the Federal Reserve to a Central Ledger Authority (CLA).

A CLA is not technically a bank but serves in the role of a banking referee and scorekeeper. It does not hold any reserves, but they are aggregated in the deposits in corresponding banks. The accounting role of the CLA is two-fold. First, to keep a ledger with the correspondent banks that hold savings deposits and issue loans. Secondly, it can manage the currency supply based on stable formulas focused on the growth of median household wealth rather than GDP. It will issue money to the correspondent banks that need it for fractional-reserve lending, which is the mechanism for organic economic growth.

This integral system is rooted in the spontaneous economic relations described in the previous chapter. We can understand elements of integral banking institutions through a brief history of banking regulations that serve individuals, the development of fractional reserve lending, and problems with state/central bank cabals that need reform.

## Banks Of Deposit And Exchange

The original purpose of banks was to safely store money. Gold and silver were heavy, and only limited amounts could be carried around. Supplies were placed in guarded vaults, and banks charged depositors a storage fee. These storage banks are called banks of deposit. It was unethical for storage banks to use deposits for lending or speculation because it was not their money. The banker promised to keep money or other precious objects safe for the owner. Safety deposit boxes in modern banks perform this function.

Lending money began as a separate business. Moneylenders lent their own money, which the borrower repaid with agreed-upon interest. However, many banks holding money on deposit for their customers were tempted to lend or invest it when the depositor wasn't using it. When modern banking began in Italy, some bankers unethically used a portion of the stored money for lending or other investments, keeping enough reserves to pay depositors when requested. This was a form of theft, and the depositor might not get back exactly the same coins or gold bars. When bankers were caught cheating, depositors would make a run on the bank to withdraw their deposits, causing the bank to fail. Depositors late to the bank might lose their money.

In 1361, the Venetian Senate passed a law to stop this behavior, declaring bank use of deposits illegal. The regulation made the government a referee, making banking safer for individuals. However, some bankers risked ignoring the law because secret lending of others' money was highly profitable. Some of these dishonest bankers outspent the needed reserves and went bankrupt. Then, in 1524, the government created a board of bank examiners to inspect banks to make sure all the deposits remained in storage. Bank examiners remain an important part of banking today. This is another referee function.

Bank examiners can be tempted by bribes from bankers. Despite examination laws, in 1584, the largest bank in Italy, the house of Pisano and Tiepolo, failed when it was unable to pay depositors from reserves. The Venetian government responded by establishing a state bank in 1587, the *Banco della Piazza di Rialto*, which was not allowed to make loans. The bank was allowed to earn money only from fees for services: coin storage, currency exchange, transfers between customers, and notary services.[1] Bank employees earned only wages and could not profit from lending capital. This was honest deposit banking.

Because the *Banco della Piazza di Rialto* was trustworthy, the paper notes it issued, backed by deposits, became a stable ledger currency more dependable than the coins that contained uncertain levels of purity. An honest, functional, and stable deposit banking system had been established. The *Banco della Piazza di Rialto* was a public service agency paid to protect deposits. The employees earned wages through service fees, while deposits were kept in the vault. The laws treated individual depositors as sovereign owners, as an integral economy requires.

The Bank of Amsterdam (1609) was modeled on the *Banco della Piazza di Rialto* as a secure bank of deposit and exchange. The bank supported Amsterdam's growth as a global center of trade after Antwerp fell to Spain in 1585. Growth was fueled by the invention of the joint stock company, the first stock exchange, religious freedom and openness,

---

1. John Kenneth Galbraith, *Money: Whence It Came, Where It Went* (Princeton University Press, 2017, first published 1976), p. 19.

migrating merchants, and its strategic shipping location. The bank was highly trusted, and the Dutch Guilder became the reserve currency of Europe from the mid-1600s to the late 1700s.

Banking was secure when individual deposits were guaranteed. This system enabled a spontaneous economic order. Deposits were available to owners whenever needed. The *Banco della Piazza di Rialto* and the Bank of Amsterdam performed these functions well, and their cities prospered. Banking laws, auditing processes, and stiff penalties helped secure these banks. These banks were refereed.

Eventually, these banks became compromised when governments and corporations tempted or forced them to become players. This made them less trustworthy. In Venice, the *Banco del Giro* was created as a tool to monetize the government's floating debt. It was a fiscal agent for the Republic, but displaced the *Banco della Piazza di Rialto* in the 1630s. Like printing fiat money, it made new ledger entries to accommodate Venetian public finances and wars. It had to suspend convertibility from 1648 to 1666 to fund a war, and, after that, the value of coins was debased. Convertibility was again suspended from 1714 to1739.

The Bank of Amsterdam was compromised when it violated its own rules and lent money to the Dutch East India Company, which had been granted the right to wage war by the government. The Company lost ships and merchandise and could not repay its loans. The Bank of Amsterdam became technically bankrupt and lost reserve currency status soon after.

In conclusion, a form of integral or ethical banking, limited to the roles of banks of deposit and exchange, was developed in Venice and Amsterdam with strict rules that regulated their behavior. However, when banks engaged in lending and governments became players, sound banks failed. These are problems of institutional capture or unethical governance. Michael Hudson refers to this as capture by the "rentier class."[2]

We have not yet discussed the role of banks in lending, but like ethical deposit banking, lending must also be ethical. Medieval banking

---

2. Michael Hudson, "Why Are Rent and the "Rentier Class" Crucial to What's Wrong with the Economy?" Robinson's Podcast Clips, Dec. 25, 2023. https://www.youtube.com/watch?v=npnd5owIKkw

focused on deposit and exchange and never developed an ethical framework for lending. What history teaches is that lending to governments and institutions is risky. They are objective frameworks, not subjective responsible agents. Like deposit and exchange banking, bank lending should focus on responsible individual borrowers and an ethical institutional framework.

## Fractional-Reserve Lending

Despite the unethical history of fractional-reserve lending, when ethical, it is a process that can support stable economic growth better than a gold standard or any other central controls. It needs to become an honest and regulated process that organically serves the spontaneous economic order.

Fractional reserve lending legally enables banks to lend large amounts of money while only keeping a fraction of its value on reserve. This is possible because, under normal conditions, depositors do not all withdraw their deposits at the same time, and keeping only a fraction, 10 percent or 20 percent, on deposit will be enough to meet normal withdrawals. The otherwise "idle" money on deposit can be used for productive purposes that create new assets and expand the economy.

Bank lending regulation has lagged behind bank deposit regulation because deposits were secured by forbidding lending. Unregulated lending leads to loan-sharking, speculation, unprotected deposits, and other high-risk behavior like lending to governments for war. Improperly regulated fractional reserve lending, with governments and central banks as players, leads to unstable economic growth, high inflation, and systemic collapse.

Early fractional reserve lending legislation was developed in 1668 by the Swedish Riksdag (parliament) when the Stockholm bank failed after lending without adequate reserves in 1663. The new Riksbank was structured in two parts to reduce risks: an exchange bank that held non-interest-bearing deposits backed by nearly 100 percent metal reserves, and a lending bank that accepted interest-bearing deposits and loaned against collateral or future earnings. The bank survives today as the oldest central bank, although is has suffered some runs and collapses that led to better regulation. It has added deposit insurance, enhanced banking supervision. a lender-of-last-resort function, and other tools. Other central banks adopted fractional-reserve lending because it works smoothly as a natural process of money expansion not strictly tied to existing assets. The United States adopted it in 1791.[3]

Fractional-reserve lending enables the creation of "new money" through debt financing of future asset production. When a loan is used for a productive enterprise, like building a house or a factory, assets are added to the economy, causing expansion. Fractional reserve lending in an ethical framework does not create inflation because the "new money" matches the growth of new economic assets.

Inflation is the result of lending for a non-productive purpose, like most government spending, when new money is injected into the economy without producing any new assets. A bank cannot give out lots of free money and stay in business, but governments print fiat money for non-productive purposes, inflating the money supply and causing a hidden tax on individuals. This is essentially counterfeiting. The spontaneous economic order is weakened by such centralized meddling.

When a government becomes a player, using the central bank for itself, rather than as a referee, it creates an unethical economic framework. Legislators should reform this, but have not withstood pressure from central banks and bureaucrats. The injustices created by the current banking systems are due to social institutions hijacking an otherwise ethical lending process serving the spontaneous economic order.

The central control of fractional-reserve banking today is a holdover from mercantilism. In an integral economy, new money enters the economy through decentralized fractional-reserve lending used for the production of new assets.

---

3. "A simple guide to fractional reserve banking," CORO. https://coro.global/blog/a-simple-guide-to-fractional-reserve-banking/

## Fractional-Reserve Lending Returns

Prior to 2020, a 10 percent reserve was required for U.S. banks. For a traditional home loan, a 10 percent reserve and FDIC insurance are required of the bank. On a $500,000, 30-year home mortgage, at 5 percent interest, the total interest earned is about $466,000, or an average of $ 15,500 per year. The origination cost of the loan to the bank is $7,000-$12,000, with about 10-30 hours of direct labor ($300-$1,000), and technology is reducing these costs.[4] It costs about $4,000 to manage the loan over its lifetime. This leaves a $450,000 profit on the loan. This loan returns an average of $15,000 annually on a $50,000 deposit. That is a 30 percent return.

Returns on commercial loans are much higher. A typical commercial 5/25 loan is 8 percent amortized over 25 years, with a balloon payment after five years. A $500,000 loan will generate $192,915 in interest for the bank during that five-year period. A $50,000 reserve will generate an average of $38,583 per year or 77 percent interest. These are enormous returns that most individuals cannot imagine. Such commercial loans generate more than double the return on capital than home mortgages.

Banking laws are written so that today the bank deposits are owned by the banks, not the depositors. This means that the owners and shareholders of banks take the 30 to 77 percent loan interest, and pay the depositors 3 to 4 percent, hardly receiving enough to keep up with inflation. It would be more ethical and lead to greater distribution of wealth if the deposits remained the property of the depositors and they received at least 50 percent of the interest their deposits generated. However, recent banking laws have led to greater centralization, not less.

## Post-2005 and COVID Centralization

Chapter 3 showed why previous centralized economies have failed to serve the spontaneous needs of individuals. A government-declared

4. Freddie Mac, "2024 Cost to Originate Study," https://sf.freddiemac.com/docs/pdf/cost-to-originate-full-study-2024.pdf

gold standard never matched gold quantities with economic needs. The Federal Reserve amplified economic crises rather than cushioning them. President Reagan's supply-side economic reforms distributed capital income to Wall Street tycoons, not workers and average citizens. What happened after 2005 was an attempt by the government and the financial industries to cobble together an institutional system based on more centralized control.

Congress first passed the Financial Services Regulatory Relief Act of 2006, which went into effect at the time of the 2008 financial crisis. This Act enables banks to park their reserves with the Fed and get paid interest through the Federal Reserve's Interest on Reserve Balances (IORB) program. The Fed currently pays banks 3.65 percent interest on these reserves. It is about the same as if they purchased treasuries, but the number of treasuries that can be issued is limited.

The IORB program enables the banks to make a profit and stay solvent without making any productive loans. The big banks currently pay 0.01 percent to 0.05 percent APY on money they can electronically park with the Fed for IORB payments. They get 3.6 percent for not lending, giving them less incentive to make regular loans.

When the COVID-19 pandemic arrived in 2020, government relief checks were sent to individuals who could not work and businesses that were forced to close. These checks increased individual bank accounts and swelled reserves at the Fed. On March 26, 2020, the Fed reduced reserve requirement ratios to 0 percent. Banks still hold reserves for liquidity, risk management, and to earn interest on reserves (IORB), but there is no fractional reserve minimum for corresponding banks. The Fed stated that its centrally held reserves are more than adequate to free up liquidity for lending by member banks.

This highly centralized system is based on the Federal Reserve serving banks, not individuals. It does not serve the economic autonomy of individuals. Economic systems and institutions arose for this. When they prioritize their own survival above serving individuals, they cause a disconnect between the entire banking system and its social usefulness. The solution is not the elimination of central institutions, but in making them ethical frameworks that act as referees, not players.

Let's consider a decentralized system in which individual banks engage in fractional-reserve lending on Main Street. All reserves are held by individuals and banks; the central ledger authority holds none. With fractional reserve percentages over 20 percent, and deposit insurance on top of that, the system becomes stable and ethical. Fractional-reserve lending can be a good mechanism for organic growth, and in a binary economy, that growth should be distributed.

## Printing Money can Be Centralized

A central agency needs to referee the printing and distribution of the national currency, and maintain ledgers with the corresponding banks. This activity does not require the central bank to hold any reserves, buy any government securities, control any interest rates, or be a player in any way. It just needs to administer rules related to the currency supply.

Thousands of corresponding banks can hold reserves and maintain insurance policies to protect their depositors in case of failure. With thousands of personal banks competing for business, and caps on bank size, no bank would be too big to fail or require a government bailout. In such a decentralized banking system, the government gets money from a central bank, but has to pay its bills through transparent public tax revenue or loans for productive activities.

In the United States, the individual states do not print money and must balance their budgets. The founders envisioned a decentralized system of states with their own religious. cultural, and economic institutions. However, in Section 8 of the Constitution, it states the federal government will coin and regulate money:

> To coin money, regulate the value thereof, and of foreign coin, and fix the standard of weights and measures;
>
> To provide for the punishment of counterfeiting the securities and current coin of the United States;

The central creation of money would serve the function of interstate commerce and eliminate the confusion caused by numerous issuers of money, as Europe had experienced. The Coinage Act of 1792 tied the value of coins to precious metals. In Chapter 3, on money, the problems of boom and bust that this created are discussed.

Section 8 says that the federal government should punish counterfeiting, and its printing for non-productive purposes is a form of counterfeiting that violates the spirit of the Constitution, even if it is called "legal tender." There is too much moral hazard when a central bank can lend new money to a government. This means that correspondent banks serve economic players, and the central bank should become an impartial exchange mechanism based on a ledger.

## Distribution To Corresponding Banks

The most stable and efficient economic system has the reserves dispersed widely through the deposits of millions of individuals in thousands of personal-level banks. This corresponds to Adam Smith's observation that pure competition is based on the maximum number of buyers and sellers. In pure competition, there is no excess profit, and the market provides efficiency. Higher market competition in banking leads to higher interest returns on deposits and lower interest rates on loans

A central bank that holds reserves acts as a monopoly and is inefficient and unstable. Banks too big to fail act as cartels. They do not serve individuals or society as a whole. Central control of an economy by a Federal Reserve chairman is like the rule of a state by a king, or a religion by a Pope or Supreme Leader. Economic rule by the people requires reforms that convert subjective leadership of a central bank into an objective framework with a currency ledger. This also eliminates a central pot of fiat money for special interests and political parties to fight over.

Fractional reserve lending from reserves distributed across all banks ensures the entire economy doesn't experience a major shock. Today, a single big bank is allowed to control up to 10 percent of the country's deposits[5] and a bank is allowed to lend up to 15 percent of its capital to

5. H. Rodgin Cohen, et. al., "Sullivan & Cromwell discusses Concentration Limits on Large Financial Companies" Columbia Law School's Blog on Corporations and the Capital Markets, December 3, 2014. https://clsbluesky.law.columbia.edu/2014/12/03/sc-discusses-concentration-limits-on-large-financial-companies/

one borrower.[6] These limits enable the largest banks to create cartels and allow too little competition and too much instability.

If 15 percent of resources are loaned to one borrower, and that borrower goes bankrupt, the bank is likely to fail. A more rational guardrail against centralization might be that no bank holds more than 5 percent of all national deposits, and no bank lends more than 5 percent of its capital to one borrower. This distribution reduces the risk of failure both for an individual bank and for the entire economy.

## A Central Ledger Authority

States can still issue an official currency if banking is decentralized. The main point is that in an ethical economic framework, the central authority should be a referee, not a player. The *Banco della Piazza di Rialto* functioned as a referee until it was superseded by the *Banco del Giro,* which was a player. The Bank of Amsterdam served as a referee until it secretly became a player. These banks did not lend.

Lending is a legitimate function of a banking system, and fractional-reserve lending can serve as a seamless basis for economic expansion when used for the creation of new assets. But this needs to be regulated by an institutional referee that is not a player who can throw the game. Banks of deposit and exchange successfully used ledgers and strict accounting rules to prevent the institutional abuse of deposits. This should also be the basis for lending money. An accounting firm does not own the money of the institutions it audits, and neither should the central money ledger authority own the money it referees for actual banks.

In an integral banking system, banks can both hold deposits and engage in lending. However, the central authority should not be called a bank, but a name that describes its actual function as a monetary authority. A central ledger authority, acting as a referee, should not own any reserves, securities, or notes. It should not lend, even as a last resort. It

6. Julia Kagan, "Understanding Bank Legal Lending Limits: Key Rules and Guidelines," Investopedia, updated November 02, 2025 https://www.investopedia.com/terms/l/legal-lending-limit.asp

would not set interest rates; it would not be a player. Protection against failure can be left to the FDIC or other insurer, and the spontaneous rescue action by other banks. A decentralized banking system as we have described will protect against a system failure so long as the central money authority is honest and accurate.

A central ledger authority would put an end to government counterfeiting of money by fiat, because it would not buy or hold any government securities or engage in any financial exchanges with the government—only banks. All banking activities would be conducted by the banks that are players, following sound banking practices that are already known.

The Federal Reserve Bank is an anachronistic, mercantilist institution. In a world of responsible individuals, a decentralized and well-regulated banking system should facilitate economic opportunities for all. Some core aspects of a central ledger authority for an integral banking system, where institutions serve individual moral agents who desire to pursue life, liberty, and happiness, are as follows:

Reserves are decentralized and held by banks. For stability, no bank should hold more than a small percentage of national deposits and loans.

Formulas related to an annual new money supply cap will not be calibrated to GDP (Gross Domestic Product), which is a centralized target, but to NGCP (nominal GDP) per capita. This formula focuses on the growth of household income while adjusting for population size.

Triennial "median net worth checks" can serve as secondary adjustments as needed. These are numbers already available.

Corresponding bank regulation tightened to limit bad loans and compounding of fractional reserve banking:

1. Begin with banks holding 35 percent reserves, and adjust with triennial checks.
2. Banks must hold all loans they originate for a minimum of five years to encourage responsible lending.
3. Banks must not lend more than a few percent of their loans to a single borrower.

4. Banks must have FDIC or similar deposit insurance.
5. A seven-year period from the transition of the Federal Reserve to the Central Ledger Authority can allow corresponding banks to build reserves and the Federal Reserve to dissolve them.
6. The dollar will remain at its current value as the transition begins, and inflation and deflation adjustment caps will be built into the new system.
7. The new money supply will expand based on safe and generally productive loans throughout a decentralized banking system. There is no national debt financing interest attached or a hidden inflation tax through fiat printing.

The combination of a starting 35 percent reserve requirement and the annual currency cap is conservative, compared to fractional reserve requirements of zero today, 10 percent in the recent past, or 20 percent in the distant past. However, this still allows adequate credit expansion for corporate and business loans to support increased production—prioritizing family growth, while generating a stable tax base sufficient for national goals like space exploration. This proposal also ends the possibility that some banks will become too big to fail.

Appendix A at the end of this book, the Decentralized Banking and Currency Stability Act, is an Act that can be presented to Congress to implement these changes.[7]

---

7. This Act was prepared by Grok/X-AI based on the parameters and principles provided for an integral banking system above.

# Part 3

## Corporations and Shareholding

# Chapter 5

## Corporations

### Joint Ventures as a Spontaneous Order

Corporations and shareholding, like money and banking, have roots in antiquity. Forms of joint ventures, in trade, expeditions, and other group activities, required many participants who desired shared risk and rewards. They can be found in ancient Mesopotamia, India, China, and Rome. These activities involved both active and passive investing. Money was a spontaneous order that facilitated these ventures, but such ventures might be considered another form of spontaneous economic institution.

Joint ventures evolved from the 11th century in Venice and other places where commerce and banking flourished. There is a recorded transfer of a one-eighth share of Copper Mountain, owned by the Stora company in Sweden, in 1288. Around 1350, tradable shares were used to divide ownership of the Bazacle Milling Company of Toulouse, France.

The joint-stock company is the forerunner of modern corporations like the Dutch East India Company, chartered in 1602. The Amsterdam Stock Exchange was formalized about 1611 to facilitate the purchase and trading of shares. Such companies, including the Virginia Company, proliferated in the 17th and 18th centuries for trade with colonies. They focused on foreign exploration and trading and were mercantilist companies, being government-chartered and granted state monopolies.

Industrial companies for mining and manufacturing had different origins. They needed fixed capital for infrastructure: buildings, machines, and water power. They were less common until the 19th century, when new technologies required large capital investments.

When the US was formed, individual states had the authority to grant charters, and laws developed to make the registration of corporations easier. In 1811, New York allowed groups of five or more, investing capital of $100,000 or less, to form manufacturing corporations. By the 1860s, most states had incorporation laws, often related to specific sectors. This facilitated the U.S. industrial revolution, developing textile mills, railroads, steel companies, and other industries without lobbying for state charters.

The Joint Stock Companies Act 1844 (Gladstone's Act) was landmark British legislation that made general incorporation possible through a simple administrative process rather than a special royal charter. These corporations had a separate legal identity from their owners.

## Democratization Of Ownership

The public trading of shares makes possible the democratization of ownership of corporations, providing more capital than can be raised privately. This capital can fund very large capital-intensive projects that had previously required years of government lobbying and strong political connections. Unlike banking and money, which governments and central banks have more tightly controlled, the Joint Stock Companies Act made wider distribution of corporate ownership possible. This can be viewed as an integral legal reform that facilitates binary income for everyone.

However, tax and other laws still exist that tend to centralize the capital income generated by corporations, so the widespread payment of dividends is curtailed. These include both state usurpation of profits and legal advantages devised by the wealthy to facilitate the consolidation of capital. Reforms are necessary to make the economic framework related to the distribution of capital income more ethical. But publicly traded stock enables individual participation and revenue sharing in capitalist production and enables individual moral agents to pursue economic autonomy in a binary economy.

## Corporations and the Distribution of Wealth

Corporations are institutional vehicles that can distribute wealth to individual shareholders, who become owners of capitalist production. As in the case of banking, the laws regulating corporations affect whether capital profits are captured centrally by institutions or widely distributed among individuals. Wide distribution is the goal of an integral economy, with the maximum number of responsible individuals on the economic playing field.

Unethical laws enable corporate profits to be hijacked by the government and the wealthy. Lower- and middle-class investors are denied capital income as a path to economic autonomy. This centralized system prompted Yuval Harari to argue: "We just don't need the vast majority of the population."[1] Alternatively, Marx and Engels argued we didn't need the bourgeoisie:

> The proletariat will use its political supremacy to wrest, by degrees, all capital from the bourgeoisie, to centralize all instruments of production in the hands of the State, i.e., of the proletariat organized as the ruling class...[2]

In an integral economy, the ownership of corporations should be as widely held as possible, not by the state or an economic class. All people, having inalienable rights to the pursuit of happiness, should have an opportunity to profit from investment in capital ownership, and from the fruits of their labor. Binary economic theory requires the widespread distribution of wealth from ownership of both one's labor and capital. This can occur when corporate profits are widely distributed to shareholders as dividends. Dividend distribution was higher before the creation of the Federal Reserve system. This process needs to be reformed.

---

1. Robert Kraychik. "WEF Adviser Yuval Harari: 'We Just Don't Need the Vast Majority of the Population' in Today's World."
2. Karl Marx and Friedrich Engels, *Manifesto of the Communist Party* (1848), trans. Samuel Moore (1888), chapter 2.

## Dividend Distribution and Corporate Taxation

The current corporation dividend payment and government taxation framework is unethical. Corporate tax laws prevent most production income from reaching shareholders. First, the government tries to intercept profits through corporate taxes before profits go to shareholders. This incentivizes corporations to show no profit to avoid paying taxes. They spend billions on tax preparation, tax evasion, reports, and frivolous spending unrelated to production. U.S. businesses spend an estimated $120 billion per year on tax compliance and avoidance. When corporations show no profit, there is nothing to distribute as dividends. This process thwarts the widespread distribution of capital income to individuals.

### Eliminate Corporate Income Tax

It is unethical for one impersonal institution to tax or own another. That makes them a player rather than a referee. Individuals are the subjective social players and should be the owners. Instead of taxing the institution, the corporation, governments should tax the shareholders, who are the owners. This enables greater dividend payments to individuals, who might be lower- or middle-class workers. The government can still receive taxes, but in the form of taxes paid by individual owners.

Taxing the owners, rather than corporations, enables corporations to put all their resources into producing and selling goods, and avoid wasting billions on tax-avoidance strategies. They could produce more, earn more, and pay more dividends. When the government taxes individuals, the double-tax problem disappears, and the principled flow of money from individuals to their governments is restored. The citizens would be owners of their capital, their labor, and their government.

In 1900, there was no U. S. corporate tax, and the percentage of corporations paying dividends was 70- 80 percent, with an average annual yield of 5-7 percent. This was higher than bank interest and in addition to the speculative value of the stock. Most investors bought stocks for dividend income. By 2020, only 20 percent of corporations paid dividends, with an annual yield averaging 1.5 percent. This was lower than bank deposit interest. When the dot-com bubble arrived in the 1990s, most new tech companies were formed without even an intent to pay dividends.

Federal corporate taxation began in 1909. The rate was 1 percent on net income exceeding $5,000. This rate began rising during WWI and peaked at 52.8 percent in 1968. Add to that an average of 4-6 percent for state taxes, and the ability to pay dividends to shareholders, or even stay in business, was greatly reduced. Dividend distribution is far less, and far less widespread than it should be, and causes economic injustice.

## Equalize Taxes on Labor and Capital Income

Economic injustice is fostered by a 20 percent rate individual income tax on dividends, while high payroll incomes are taxed at 37 percent on their wage labor. This tax differential contributes to higher ownership of shares and capital income by the wealthy. It is a form of tax haven that keeps capital ownership centralized. If both wage labor and dividend income were taxed, this unethical economic incentive would disappear.

## Require Very Large Corporations to Go Public

Private equity firms also centralize wealth by preventing the public from buying shares and accessing profits. The impersonal/personal demarcation of corporations can help ensure everyone has ownership access to very large corporations. We are recommending that large firms with a net worth of over $10 billion be required to go public. Most corporations go public before becoming that large, but including outliers could improve the decentralization of capital ownership. The economic framework would better facilitate economic autonomy.

## Mandate Dividend Payments from a Percentage of Profits

We propose that a mandatory dividend payment of 30 percent on corporate profits be made to shareholders. This would serve as a check on corporate greed. It also guarantees a wider tax base for the government to draw upon, while leaving corporations with an opportunity to reinvest a major portion of profits in research and expansion, or pay even more in dividends to shareholders. This is more than corporations currently have available, on average.

The government would not receive as large a percentage of corporate profits if the shareholders paid a 30 percent tax rate on 30 percent of dividends. This is about an 8 percent indirect tax versus 21 percent direct tax currently. However, this amount would significantly increase because:

- Many corporations would pay more dividends than the 30 percent floor. Mature firms invest less in R&D.
- Corporate profits and the overall economy will increase when millions aren't spent on tax avoidance.
- More distribution of capital wealth means less need for government social services.

Governments should be better able to balance budgets with an ethical capital distribution system that serves the economic autonomy of all citizens. The tax income stream will be more stable when distributed over a wide base.

## Conclusion

The idea of joint-stock companies is a spontaneous human activity that evolved to make capital-intensive mass production possible and drastically reduce the cost of consumer goods. However, unethical laws and institutional frameworks have led to the centralization of the wealth produced by these companies. We have proposed policies for an ethical economic framework that would democratize capitalism and enable everyone to prosper from both their labor and capital value. It would eliminate direct corporate income tax, but mandate a 30 percent corporate dividend payout.

We have developed proposed legislation in the Shareholder Dividend and Corporate Tax Reform Act[3] attached as Appendix 2.

3. This bill was prepared by Grok/X-AI based on the parameters and principles we provided for an ethical corporation and tax framework above.

# Chapter 6

## *Financial Services*

In Chapter 4, on integral banking, we noted that financial services are separate from banking. Banking involves deposits, lending, and currency exchange. Financial services involve advising, brokerage, capital formation, securities, underwriting, mutual funds, and insurance. These services do not create money or assets but facilitate capital ownership, reallocate risk, facilitate mergers and acquisitions, take corporations public, and provide wealth management. Service industries do not directly produce assets, goods, or economic growth, but they help people to organize capital to create growth, earn capital income, and manage their wealth.

Corporate shares are a form of money, even though they are not liquid cash. Their value depends on corporate profitability and fluctuates relative to standard currency, but they are traded for their value like other assets. There are parallels between banks managing money and financial firms managing corporate shares. Corporate shares generate dividends on profits, while bank deposits generate income on loans. There is moral hazard, or conflict of interest, when a brokerage firm uses client shares as security for their own investing, like when a bank speculates with depositor savings, when they act as a player rather than a servant.

### Wealth Centralization or Decentralization?

Centralization of wealth in the financial services sector is facilitated by unethical tax laws and regulations that provide barriers to entry. Entry barriers are created when financial services focus on wealthy clients, rather than providing their service to everyone. Giving wealthy clients first access to exclusive opportunities for high returns or personal capital management naturally concentrates wealth over time, even when everyone technically has access to markets.[1]

The highest returns come from private placements, hedge funds, venture capital, private equity, and other investments unavailable to most individuals. Broker-dealers tend to place only "accredited investors" in higher-return funds. SEC regulations define an accredited investor as having a net worth of greater than $1 million. This excludes over 90 percent of U.S. households from capital gains opportunities available to those already wealthy, reinforcing the centralization of capital wealth. [2]Less wealthy clients are steered to financial advisors who place money in impersonal mutual funds and on investments with higher fees. This makes it structurally more difficult for lower-income investors to earn equal returns on their capital.

The carried interest tax loophole enables private equity, hedge fund, and venture capital managers to receive approximately 20 percent of fund profits as "carried interest." Like dividends, these profits are taxed at long-term capital gains rates rather than labor income rates. Proponents argue it is a reward for risk-taking, but governments should not subsidize such risk; the increased income from the risk is the natural reward. People should be taxed on the total amount of their income, regardless of the source. Opponents have promoted the Carried Interest Fairness Act.[3]

The structure of the financial services sector does not have a central institution like the Federal Reserve, but arose more spontaneously, serving

1. James Best and Keshav Dogra "Capital Management and Wealth Inequality." *Federal Reserve Bank of New York Staff Reports,* no. 1072, September 2023; revised January 2024. https://www.newyorkfed.org/medialibrary/media/research/staff_reports/sr1072.pdf?sc_lang=en

2. Jennifer J. Schulp, "Sophistication or Discrimination? How the Accredited Investor Definition Unfairly Limits Investment Access for the Non-wealthy and the Need for Reform," Cato Institute, February 8, 2023. https://www.cato.org/testimony/sophistication-or-discrimination-how-accredited-investor-definition-unfairly-limits#

3. Introduced in the 119th Congress as H.R. 1091 and S. 445

a wide variety of fragmented purposes. However, the Dodd-Frank Act of 2010 moved in that direction with the creation of the Financial Stability Oversight Council (FSOC), aimed at monitoring systemic risks. It has not yet become a central player. Because the financial services sector is more aligned with a spontaneous order serving individual needs, there is less need for macroeconomic structural reform than in the banking sector.

However, tax policies keep capital gains concentrated among the very wealthy. Corporate tax and dividend reforms are discussed in Chapter 5, and family inheritance and other taxes are discussed in Chapter 8: Taxes on Income and Inheritance.

## Brokerage Firm Collapses

Current laws enable the brokerage firms to be the "legal owner," while the individual who purchases the share is called the "beneficial owner." This legal framework enables the broker to become a player with individuals' shares. By agreement, often in fine print, stock brokers can legally use client shares in authorized ways to make profits for themselves by collateralizing client assets as leverage for short-term borrowing. The beneficial owner is often given a share of the returns on these speculative and more risky financial activities.

The 2008 Bear Stearns and Lehman Brothers collapses exposed clients to losses when securities they leveraged weren't promptly returned. Like bank depositors are protected by the FDIC, investors are protected by the Securities Investor Protection Act (SIPC). SIPC guarantees individual investors up to $500,000 per customer for missing securities and cash, with a sub-limit of $250,000 for cash claims. The cash limit was raised from $100,000 to $250,000 after the 2008 crisis. However, the SIPC liquidation process transferred all Lehman Brothers accounts to other firms in a fire sale.

The government facilitated the Bear Stearns acquisition by JPMorgan Chase. TARP (the Troubled Asset Relief Program) disbursed $443.5 billion and recovered all but $31 billion. Fannie Mae and Freddie Mac were placed under conservatorship with the Treasury, which paid out $190 billion, which has been recovered. The Federal Reserve provided trillions in liquidity through short-term loans and reported a profit of $2.5 billion.

The Glass-Steagall Act of 1933 separated deposit banking from the other financial industries and largely fixed those institutions until it was repealed. The SEC increased transparency, but no legislation provided prudent oversight or regulated mortgage-backed securities or collateralized debt. Had there been better guardrails on brokerage institutions, the 2008 collapse would not have happened.

To address these systemic risks, Congress passed the Dodd-Frank Wall Street Reform Act and Consumer Protection Act of 2010. Unfortunately, these Acts were written to limit the damage caused by an unethical institutional framework, but did not make the framework more ethical. It became more centralized and less ethical by imposing heavy regulatory burdens on smaller firms. This led to mergers and acquisitions, creating fewer and larger firms.

In 2007, there were 5,982 reported FINRA-registered broker-dealers. By 2023, this number had dropped to 3,394. Dodd-Frank nearly doubled the number of regulations and added over $50 billion in compliance costs to the industry. Firms with fewer than 150 registered representatives lacked the scale to cover these fixed costs. Smaller firms were forced to merge with larger firms or close.

## Financial Services as Stewardship

Our integral economic framework considers the term "Financial Industry" misleading. Industries produce goods, while the service sector helps people. "Financial services" is a more accurate term. Banks or brokerage firms should serve their clients—depositors, borrowers, and shareholders. They should be stewards of their clients' wealth and not put it at risk for their own speculation without a clear partnership agreement.

The "fine print" in agreements places an undue and unethical burden on clients. Clear labeling of services can be improved. If a broker is going to leverage the legal ownership of shares, it is better to label it as a leveraged account offering higher, riskier returns than a burdensome "opt-out" clause buried in fine print. Clear marking of each financial service can be improved.

In an integral economy, the goal is to make unethical financial institutions ethical. There should be clear laws that level the playing field and are easily understood by everyone. In a binary economy, everyone should be able to receive an income from both labor and capital, so the services that help individuals receive income from capital need to be servants and referees, not manipulators.

## Personal and Impersonal Financial Institutions

The distinction between personal and impersonal financial institutions is diagrammed in Figure 2 (Chapter 2). Personal financial services, like the parents in a family, help individuals gain autonomy and pursue happiness. Impersonal services, like online stock purchases, need to be governed by ethical frameworks that serve everyone the same, without picking favorites or cronies.

The body of society is the day-to-day relations of individuals, who are the players producing, buying, selling, investing, and engaging in other economic activities. These activities should be served by personal financial institutions and framed and refereed by impersonal ones. Unethical financial frameworks generally confuse these functions. Lobbyists by large firms continually ask Congress to rig the game in their favor, making the playing field uneven. They fund political parties to do their bidding.

Individuals often ask impersonal institutions to provide personal care. A state can only assign you a number and give you a form, but a seasoned broker can provide personal financial care. Your broker can understand your financial situation and understand which investments help you with your financial goals. We expect he will exercise good moral agency. An online investment account with a big firm is impersonal; you study different stocks and funds and make a choice. Their job is to facilitate the transaction you requested and to provide correct information. If they do that, they are an ethical framework.

Impersonal institutions have abstract relationships with individuals. They should be considered as frameworks, not actors. They operate on rules and procedures. They don't physically see, hear, or touch their clients. They know what appears in a database or is on a form, but have no sense of whether it is true without additional information about the person, and stiff penalties when they are caught lying.

Let's use the example of a home loan. If an individual gets a loan from a local community banker, the borrower meets a banker face to face. The banker gets an impression of the borrower's honesty that a computer reading a database in New York cannot know. The borrower also forms a personal impression of the bank based on its appearance, professionalism, and attention to detail. The banker, who works and lives in the community, can drive by the house and look at it, and develop a better opinion of its value than a computer in New York comparing prices of recent sales in the area.

The impersonal lender may be able to operate with greater efficiency and lower overhead costs, reducing the price of the loan, but this comes with moral hazard. The 2008 financial crisis illustrated that hazard. Originating banks wrote risky mortgages because they could turn around and sell them to a Wall Street firm and shift the risk onto an impersonal firm. When thousands of these risky loans were used by big firms as collateral, the system broke.

Eliminating this type of moral hazard is important for an integral economy. This is why our Decentralized Banking and Currency Stability Act (Appendix 2) states:

> Each originating bank shall retain at least 50 percent (or the full term, whichever is shorter) of every loan it originates for a minimum of five years. Securitization or sale before this period is prohibited except in FDIC-supervised resolution.

Being required to assume some financial responsibility for mortgages one writes should be obvious. It greatly reduces the moral hazard.

Impersonal institutions are easily gamed, as we can see with Social Security checks going out to dead people, poverty programs used for money laundering, and fears about mail-in-ballot counting. Financial services are as susceptible to fraud as any impersonal institution. The bad mortgage originations passed off to impersonal buyers are a typical example of gaming the system.

Both actions by the government and by financial institutions contributed to the economic crisis of 2007-2010. The government contributed when politicians wrote irresponsible legislation to make housing more affordable to low-income borrowers. This includes the Community Reinvestment Act (CRA) of 1977, the Federal Housing Enterprises Financial Safety and Soundness Act (FHEFSSA) (1992), HUD's National Homeownership Strategy and Related Initiatives (1995), and the American Dream Downpayment Act (ADDA) (2003).

By reducing down payment barriers and expanding federal guarantees, originators were incentivized to write riskier loans and offload them quickly on big impersonal Wall Street firms, which were incentivized to earn higher CRA ratings on loans that posed no risk to themselves. The number of risky loans exponentially escalated as scammers learned how to game this system, eventually causing systemic collapse.

The low-income people the loans were supposed to help ended up in bankruptcy instead of gaining home ownership. "The road to hell is paved with good intentions" became a freeway to hell when politicians wrote laws enabling impersonal financial institutions to be gamed by thousands of people for billions of dollars. Conservative economists blamed the government for backing risky assets. The politicians blamed the financial institutions. Both were at fault because impersonal institutions that should be fair referees were unfair players.

The low-income people who lost their homes would have been better served by laws that prohibited adjustable-rate mortgages or no-interest for three-year enticements—well-established guardrails.

## Who Guards the Guardians?

Barney Frank was chairman of the House Financial Services Committee (2007–2011), and Chris Dodd was chairman of the Senate Banking

Committee (2007–2011). Frank had received significant campaign contributions from Fannie Mae, and Dodd had received favorable "VIP" mortgages from Countrywide Financial (a subprime lender that failed in 2008). While both were cleared of direct conflict of interest in the legislation they proposed, they were fully embedded in a system that assumed financial institutions and governments could play a positive role as players rather than referees in the economy.

A paradigm shift is required, one that understands social institutions are governed by laws consistent with the integral consciousness in the "head."[4] This consciousness should have state-of-the-art knowledge of the nature of impersonal institutions, how they differ from personal institutions, and how gaming or hijacking them can be prevented.

There are many other details related to the subprime mortgage trading by big Wall Street firms that were a secondary set of risky behaviors that made previous economic bubbles possible. The Tulip Mania (1634), the South Sea and Mississippi Bubbles (1720), the 1929 Stock Market Collapse, the Japanese Asset Bubble (1986-1991), and the Dot-Com Bubble (1995-2000) all involved economic institutions with insufficient guardrails.

There is hope for reform when lessons learned about both individual moral behavior and impersonal institutional structures get embedded in the conscience of the "head," and embodied objectively in the left wing and subjectively in the right wing of society. It is that consciousness that guards the guardians.

---

4. See Figure 1, Chapter 2, "The Philosophical Framework."

# Chapter 7

## *Patent Reform*

The purpose of a patent is to incentivize people to invent new and useful products to make the lives of others better. Before the United States was founded, many colonies had different patent laws. To help the federal government regulate interstate commerce, the U.S. Founders created a unified patent system through the Constitution. Article I, Section 8, Clause 8):

> To promote the Progress of Science and useful Arts, by securing for limited Times to Authors and Inventors the exclusive Right to their respective Writings and Discoveries.

Congress has the authority to pass patent laws within this general framework. The patent term was initially 14 years, in 1861 raised to 17 years, and in 1995 raised to 20 years from the filing date. The patent must be filed by an individual (natural person). The filer can transfer the rights to a corporation or other institution.

Thomas Jefferson thought that ideas belonged to everyone and was worried that patents would create monopolies on products that would hinder rather than advance progress. As a compromise, the founders agreed that all the ideas related to producing the invention be explained in the patent filing. Then, when the patent expires and enters the public domain, others can produce it competitively.

Results have been mixed. Patents stimulate invention, but they are also used for price gouging and other mischief. Transferring them to institutions tends to increase this mischief because institutions are objective frameworks with profit goals, not moral subjects with a conscience. These are a few ways the current patent system can be gamed:

1. The patent system can be used to price-gouge consumers. For example, a medicine invented to cure a disease that costs $2.00 to produce can be sold for $1,000 because of the monopoly status provided by the patent. This would harm low-income people who might die because they cannot afford the medicine.
2. A patent holder can increase planned obsolescence by producing a product that has a short lifespan and has to be continually repurchased.
3. Companies can buy a new patent from the inventor and then withhold production in order to continue earning more money from their inferior existing products.
4. Pharmaceutical "evergreening" involves slightly changing the formulation and filing a secondary patent to continue the monopoly after the original patent expires.

These unethical practices usually involve institutions that hold patents to avoid competition and exploit individual consumers rather than serve them. Individuals are more likely to act with conscience.

One notable example of a moral individual is Jonas Salk, who invented the polio vaccine and put the patent in the public domain. He thought the vaccine was so important it should be inexpensively available to everyone. Salk's was also inspired because his research was significantly funded by the March of Dimes campaign, which collected pennies and dimes in boxes at schools and elsewhere.

## Compulsory Royalty Licensing

This patent system can be easily reformed to eliminate price gouging, shelving, and other gaming of the system. This can be accomplished by introducing a system that combines spontaneous competition for market efficiency with a windfall reward for the inventor. This is compulsory royalty licensing. Here is how it works.

The patent holder must allow others to produce the product with a mandatory royalty payment of 10 percent of sales to the patent holder. With many producers competing, the product would sell for the market price of a generic plus the 10 percent fee that had to be paid to the patent holder. The patent holder would receive a windfall whether he produced the product or not. Consumers would pay 10 percent more than a generic and not get price-gouged.

The information in the patent filing is public knowledge, so everyone has access to it. No extra work on behalf of the patent holder would be required. Furthermore, 1099-MISC tax forms already exist for royalty payments. All producers would have to send these forms to the patent holder and the IRS. This will simplify accounting and ensure compliance. This compulsory royalty licensing system addresses both Thomas Jefferson's desire that ideas be free and that monopolies, shelving, and price-gouging be prevented. This system falls within the constitutional framework and only requires changes to the patent laws from Congress.

## Government Funding of Patents

A second problem with the current patent system involves government funding. Photos taken by NASA are put in the public domain because they were paid for by the government, and the individuals who work on the photographs are on a government salary. However, if the government gives a grant to a university or a corporation, should they be able to obtain a patent and use it for price gouging? The taxpayer first pays for the grant and then gets charged an exorbitant price for the product.

The profits from COVID-19 vaccines stand in stark contrast to the polio vaccine. The United States government invested at least $31 billion dollars through Operation Warp Speed, with over $18 billion going to Moderna. Pfizer/BioNTech received about $445 million from the German government. The underlying mNRA research had already received hundreds of millions of dollars in grants in previous decades.

Moderna and Pfizer/BioNTech hold patents on their mRNA vaccines. They produced the vaccines for $1-3 per dose and sold them to governments for $15-40 per dose. Then they raised prices 4 to 5 times more on the boosters, which many considered gouging. Medicare Part B paid $161.65 for the Moderna Spikevax booster and $155.90 for the Pfizer Comirnaty booster. Those without insurance were charged $140-$250 at pharmacies. Together, these companies generated over $100 billion in vaccine sales revenue.

While most individuals paid nothing directly for the shots, they indirectly paid through increased health insurance prices, rising government debt, and inflation. Patent law reforms can greatly reduce this problem of corporations profiting from government grants.

This problem began 45 years ago. Before 1980, the government held the patent on inventions developed with federal grants. However, the government, with no subjective consciousness, let thousands of discoveries go undeveloped. Bureaucrats lacked the incentive, expertise, or budget to produce them. It was a terrible waste. Only a fraction of these patents ever benefited society.

The Bayh-Dole Act of 1980 addressed this problem of government-shelved patents by allowing grant recipients to patent and profit from their government-funded inventions. In return, the government receives a royalty-free, non-exclusive license to use the invention for its own purposes. The Bayh-Dole Act led to more products being produced, but the price-gouging exemplified by the COVID-19 vaccine prices followed. This has substantially driven up health care and other costs.

A compulsory licensing policy would eliminate this price-gouging. However, in medicines, more producers needing FDA approval cause greater approval bottlenecks, which are currently at 18-30 months. This could be addressed with an additional compulsory royalty fee, starting at about 2 percent, specifically to speed up FDA approval.

## Government Share of Royalties

One final issue is a resolution to the question of the government's share of royalty fees. The pre-1980 policies did not work because government patents sat on shelves. The Bayh-Dole Act gave the government lower procurement prices but no royalty share, and it opened the floodgates for unethical pricing.

This can be fixed by having the government receive a share of profits from the patent to help fund future research. A grant proposal could contain an agreed-upon government share of royalties in exchange for providing the grant. For example, if the grant was expected to cover 40 percent of the research and development costs, that percentage could be included in the grant agreement. It is best if the percentage is negotiated up front to avoid lawsuits and haggling over final costs later. This approach balances the weaknesses of both the pre-1980 approach and the consequences of the Bayh-Dole Act.

## Conclusion

We are proposing legislation to reform patent law to remove unethical aspects of the framework and make it consistent with an integral economy. The proposed Patent Reform and Public Access Act[1] (Appendix 3) would lead to systemic improvements in the economy generally, but particularly noticeable in the reduction of health care costs inflated by corporations gaming the current patent law system.

1. Written with the help of Grok X/AI which was fed the proposed reforms outlined above.

# Part 4

# Integral Distribution of Wealth

# Chapter 8

## *Taxes on Income and Inheritance*

Taxes are a fundamental aspect of any economy. They always affect individuals' incentives and institutional frameworks. There is an old market truism often taught in introductory economics that goes something like this:

> The more you tax something, the less of it you get. The more you subsidize something, the more of it you get.

Tax policies affect the centralization of wealth. The "Shareholder Dividend and Corporate Tax Reform Act"[1] we proposed in Chapter 5 works against the centralization of wealth caused by government taxation of corporations. This is one major area of tax reform in an integral economy. However, there are other types of taxes, such as capital gains and inheritance taxes, that need scrutiny.

### Inheritance Taxes

The centralization of wealth continues and gets amplified through the transfer of wealth via inheritance. The family is the fundamental social institution, and people naturally want to leave their assets to their children to help their economic autonomy. However, inheritance transfers keep capital concentrated among wealthy families, giving a few families significant control over the entire economy.

1. Appendix 3 contains the proposed bill text.

Family wealth concentration is currently addressed by wealth transfer taxes on very large estates, with an exemption that allows parents to provide economic security to their children. In the United States, there is a $15 million federal exemption for an estate; above that, estates are taxed at 40 percent.[2] Twelve states add their own inheritance tax, the most progressive being Oregon, with a $1 million threshold, and Connecticut has the highest with $15 million, matching the federal government. Wealthy people are incentivized to move out of those states when they retire.

There is also an inheritance tax "loophole" based on a stepped-up cost basis of assets. This includes stock transfers, homes, land, businesses, and other assets on which capital gains taxes are normally paid when they are sold. The cost basis is what an individual pays for an asset like shares. If the shares are held for years or decades, they may be worth many times the cost basis. When the individual sells the stock, a capital gains tax is paid. However, if the individual dies and the stock is transferred to an heir, the cost basis is reset to the current value. No capital gains accrued during the original owner's life are ever paid.

Government administrators complain about these asset value resets because they feel the government is getting cheated. But there is a sound reason for this reset. If an heir with no money inherits a house and has to pay capital gains on its increased value, he might have to sell the house to pay the tax. The same is true of a business.

There have been many proposals like taxing capital gains at death to close this "loophole." This might work better for stocks than other assets. Some proposals include exemptions for houses, farms, and small businesses, but they get complicated and difficult to administer. It can be argued that the current law already compensates for the step-up reset with the progressive 40 percent transfer tax on very large estates, which exceeds all capital gains tax rates.

An integral economy rests on the economic autonomy of individuals. An inheritance can contribute to that autonomy and support the heir's upward mobility. This can be viewed as a social good. We do not

2. This is the rate defined in "The One Big Beautiful Bill Act" (signed July 4, 2025).

see changing inheritance laws as having a significant effect on the distribution of wealth. If any adjustments are made, it is reasonable to tweak the wealth transfer tax rate or the exemption amount and keep this one simple form filed for estate transfers.

## Capital Gains vs. Capital Income

When discussing taxes on capital, it is important to distinguish between capital gains on assets and capital income from corporate dividends. There are good reasons to forget capital gains and focus on the earned income from capital. In addition to avoiding the step-up reset problem, there are two reasons that a capital gains tax is unethical.

First, capital gains are often a tax on phantom gains, as many of the gains taxed do not keep up with inflation. The IRS has estimated that taxing capital gains on an adjusted basis would reduce the capital gains tax revenue by about one-third.[3]

Second, capital gains taxes represent a violation of the principle related to rights, liberty, and property. A bedrock principle of the U.S. Declaration of Independence. It puts a government ownership claim on an individual's property. Critics view it as a second tax on one's labor.

A capital gains tax also affects economic efficiency by encouraging people to hold appreciated assets excessively long to avoid a tax, distorting capital markets, reducing liquidity, and preventing reallocation to higher-value uses for new ventures. This "lock-in effect" is documented.[4]

The "Shareholder Dividend and Corporate Tax Reform Act" we propose will increase tax revenue from capital income in a way that limits economic distortions and diverting capital expenditures on tax avoidance. By directly taxing corporations, the government becomes an interloper in the production cycle. By taxing individuals' dividend income, the government taxes the true owners after they have received their share

3. "Indexing Capital Gains Taxes for Inflation," Congress.gov. CRS R45229. https://www.congress.gov/crs-product/R45229

4. Shahira ElBogdady Knight "The Economic Effects of Capital Gains Taxation" Joint Economic Subcommittee, June, 1997.

of the profits. Further, by mandating dividend payments, corporations are required to respect the investment of their shareholders and treat them as owners. Finally, widespread dividend payments help decentralize wealth in the economy.

Lower- and middle-income investors will have a greater incentive to buy stocks if they see significant earnings on their capital investment. They do not see this because of (1) government interloping, and (2) unethical tax policies.

## Tax Capital and Labor Income at the Same Rate

In a binary economy with more income generated by capital than labor, everyone should be able to earn income from both. An ethical framework taxes capital income and wage income at the same rate. Those who earn more income from capital should not be taxed at a lower rate. Warren Buffett explained this in an NBC interview with Tom Brokaw in 2007, saying that he was taxed at 17.4 percent, while his secretary was taxed at32.9 percent.[5] This tax rate disparity is probably the largest tax loophole in the U.S. tax code. From the standpoint of an integral economy, a true "fair tax" taxes labor and capital income at the same rate.

By contrast, Steve Forbes proposed a "flat tax" in his 1996 and 2000 presidential campaigns that would be a 17 percent flat tax with a $13,000 exemption for adults and a $5,000 exemption per dependent child. [6]While he considered this fair and equitable, the flat tax only applied to wage income, and capital income was taxed separately and at lower rates. He failed to address the big loophole. He called his proposal a "moral case," but it only affected labor income. From a binary economics standpoint, this would not be an unethical tax.

Taxing income from capital and wages at the same rate is the best

5. *The Guardian,* Business Section, Oct. 31, 2007. https://www.theguardian.com/business/2007/oct/31/usnews

6. Steve Forbes, "The Moral Case for the Flat Tax, *Imprimis,* October, 1996. https://imprimis.hillsdale.edu/wp-content/uploads/2016/11/The-Moral-Case-for-the-Flat-Tax-October-1996.pdf

strategy to level the playing field. To be most effective for wealth distribution, this change should be coupled with our proposed Shareholder Dividend and Corporate Tax Reform Act that assures capital earnings are distributed to rightful owners. Then progressive tax brackets can help lower-income people gain economic autonomy.

## State or Federal Income Tax?

The U.S. Founders created a union of states that were to be self-sufficient and, if taxed, pay the union on an apportioned basis. Individuals did not pay federal income taxes. Article I, Section 2, Clause 3 states:

> Representatives and direct Taxes shall be apportioned among the several States which may be included within this Union, according to their respective Numbers...

The Sixteenth Amendment (1913) created an exemption allowing the federal government to directly collect income taxes from individuals to establish the Federal Reserve Bank.

An integral standpoint sees an income tax as an acceptable form of tax, because the individuals own the government. However, the government's use of the tax needs appropriate checks and balances. In the Founders' system, the states would compete with each other for residents, and therefore, the most efficient states would have lower taxes and attract more productive activities. People would vote with their feet. States would provide a check on federal spending through the Senate, which was composed of two senators appointed by each state. The Seventeenth Amendment, which said individuals would vote for senators, eliminated that primary check on state sovereignty and federal power.

The Seventeenth Amendment created a system of more direct democracy. Before 1913, states could pressure or recall senators who voted for expansive federal programs at state expense. After 1913, national issues, campaign financing, and party loyalty dominated. Two parties replaced 48 states at the federal level. The federal government became a pig trough for party donors unchecked by state senators to foster mob rule with special-interest money. The states became like provinces, following sticks and carrots that the political parties decided the federal government would provide.

An integral economy needs checks and balances on taxes at every level of government. Transparency, accountability, and straightforward methods of removing corrupt officials from office are required to safeguard the use of any public money. The Sixteenth and Seventeenth Amendments removed important checks instituted by the Founders that facilitated the hijacking of income taxes by special interests through political parties.

## Conclusion

This brief survey of the U.S. federal approach to income taxes is mixed.

On the positive side, an integral tax system should enable individuals to gain economic autonomy. A progressive income tax that exempts those below a poverty level does this. An inheritance system that allows parents to transfer a significant amount of wealth to heirs without a penalty does this. The progressive nature of the tax from 10 percent to a 37 percent cap serves the cause of wealth decentralization while not excessively punishing success. This approach is more integral than a flat tax.

On the negative side, binary income is unethically taxed. Taxing labor income at a higher rate than capital favors the capitalist and punishes the worker. By taxing corporate profits directly, the government seizes property from the shareholder-owners. It can be argued that this violates the takings clause in the Fifth Amendment to the Constitution. When institutions control other institutions, individual owners are circumvented. Taxing capital gains also falls on the negative side, because it is also a tax on the value of one's property. The tax structure needs to keep the government as a referee among individuals on the playing field. It is more principled for the purchaser to pay a sales tax on the purchase of property, rather than for the owner to pay a recurring tax on his property.

# Chapter 9

## *Tax Transactions Not Property*

Transactions describe the relationships that take place on the economic playing field. Our philosophical framework (Chapter 2) used an image of a bird with institutions on the left wing, individuals on the right wing, and relationships in the body.

**Figure 6: Integral Economy—Head, Body, Wings**

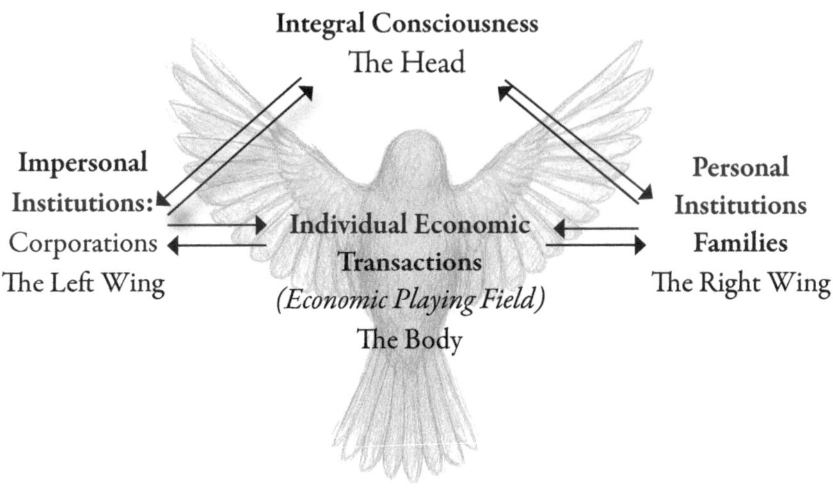


In this chapter, we use this modified diagram to focus specifically on the economic sector and make a case for taxing transactions in the body, not the wings that hold up society.

We have already made a strong case for not taxing corporations—institutions on the left wing. They serve the integral purpose of producing goods and services and providing wealth to people. If you tax production, you cause economic dysfunction. Fewer goods will be produced, there will be less income to pay workers, and less profit to pay shareholders.

A similar case can be made for taxes on individuals, which is known as capitation, head tax, or poll tax. The U.S. founders specifically addressed this in Article I, Section 9, Clause 4:

> No Capitation, or other direct, Tax shall be laid, unless in Proportion to the Census or enumeration herein before directed to be taken.

They specifically mentioned this as a direct tax, and if we return to Article I, Section 2, Clause 3, we find that direct taxes should be apportioned to the states.

A head tax is a payment on your right to exist; it violates one's inalienable rights in the Declaration of Independence. Your body is your asset, and taxing assets is a form of theft. We speak of taxing individuals and institutions because they are visible. But this is theft consciousness—we take from a thing. It is a form of foraging and pillaging.

## Transactions are Optional

Transactions are optional. Individuals are not forced to engage in them. If a tax is laid on a transaction, it is burdensome, but not mandatory. An individual can forego or postpone the transaction. There is an element of economic *dissuasion* laid on the transaction. But ultimately, the individual *voluntarily* accepts the transaction with the tax.

Income taxes are taxes on transactions. You can agree to accept a job or not accept it. You and your employer both know the tax involved and agree to accept or offer a job knowing this. Sales taxes are taxes on transactions. They are added to the purchase price of a product, and both the buyer and the seller agree on a price, having figured in the tax. The transaction is voluntary. The government has not committed an act of theft by force, because you agreed to pay the tax when you decided to buy the product. A road toll tax is not physical theft, especially if there are slower alternate routes. You have a choice to drive on the road.

Slavery is not a transaction. It is an economic activity imposed by force and differs in kind from voluntary employment. This is a form of the distinction between taxing things vs. transactions. The body of the economy is where transactions take place. The right wing raises the individuals that perform these interactions, and the left-wing institutions are impersonal structures that facilitate and regulate. You don't want to tax those institutions on either the left or the right, or they are debilitating wings of the economy. Transactions should be taxed, not things or wings.

## Property and Assets Serve Autonomy and Productivity

Individuals and corporations hold property and other assets. Property contributes to the autonomy of individuals and the productivity of a corporation. A corporation needs a building, tools, and a stock of inventory. If these things are taken, the corporation's productivity is reduced. Taxing the corporation directly is like taking a piece of the liver out of a body instead of waiting for a healthy body to hand you harvested food.

An individual requires property ownership for autonomy to pursue happiness, serve others, and engage in other economic transactions. We began this book by quoting Aristotle:

> there is this further point: there is great pleasure in giving, help friends and associates, making things easy for strangers; and this can only be done by someone who has property of his own.[1]

The U.S. founders, following John Locke, believed in the sanctity of property:

> ...nor shall any person ... be deprived of life, liberty, or property, without due process of law; nor shall private property be taken for public use, without just compensation.[2]

In the last chapter, the distinction between transactions and property was discussed in relation to capital gains taxes. A capital gain tax is a tax

1. Ch. 1, Note 1.
2. U.S. Constitution, Amendment 5, Section 1

on property, while a tax on a dividend payment is a tax on a transaction. In principle, a capital gains tax is a form of theft, but a tax on dividends is voluntarily accepted by the stock buyer when purchasing shares.

Taxes or fees on public services like water, sewer, or utilities like electricity and natural gas are transactional and justifiably turned off for lack of payment. But they do not involve confiscating your car or other asset. That becomes coercive and unethical.

An unethical tax is a license plate fee tied to the value of a car. A sales tax is paid on an automobile when it is purchased. This is a transaction tax. However, 25-30 states charge a value-based tax every year when vehicle registration is renewed. Some argue this plate tax is needed to pay for roads, but it is still a tax on an asset already taxed when it was purchased. That sales tax could go for the roads. Gas taxes pay for roads based on their use; this is more ethical. A flat registration fee that offsets administrative costs to issue a license plate or tab is most ethical.

Police confiscation of cars, cash, guns, and other property is also questionable. This is civil asset forfeiture. Many states allow police departments to keep confiscated property by claiming it is connected to a crime, even if the case never goes to court. About 16 states require a conviction before forfeiture. While police confiscation is constitutionally permitted, the system has well-documented abuse, bad incentives, and innocent victims. It needs reform. It is more principled for taxpayers to pay for the police department through a general fund, and have any confiscated property go to the general fund.

## Land Commons

When land commons are involved, taxation becomes more blurred. Cities could not deliver police, fire protection, public schools, or other necessary services without an annual fee to cover their cost. There needs to be a way for the city to collect these fees if the property owner becomes delinquent. Placing a claim on the property to assure these fees is the only way to secure payment of these common fees. Hence, a property tax.

But how should property be taxed? There is a good argument that only the land, not the building or improvements, is taxed. The cost of a fire or police call does not change whether there is a small or big house on the property. A property tax based on the value of the house is comparable to a license plate fee based on the value of a car. You are taxing owned assets, not a property transaction or a fee-for-service. The extra charge can be considered a taking.

In the 19th century, economist Henry George proposed a land value tax (LVT),[3] arguing that land value is largely created through community services and infrastructure, rather than owner improvements. He argued that traditional assessments discourage home improvements and new construction that owners would make without assessments. Georgians support building codes that promote public safety, but tend to oppose zoning laws in favor of freedom and economic development. We consider this to be a principled approach to property tax in an integral economy.

Public utilities like water, sewer, gas, and electricity can be provided by cities or other utilities for a fee based on use. Today, especially in suburban areas, cities are lagging behind private land development. Private developers create homeowner's associations (HOAs) to build roads and maintain water, sewer, and other infrastructure. In the case of townhomes and condominiums, HOA fees cover common roofing, lawn maintenance, and other community services. These fees are in addition to city taxes for police, fire, and schools.

HOAs drive up the cost of home ownership, yet they continue to expand. In 1964, there were about 500 HOAs in the United States; this rose to 10, 000 in 1970, 100,000 in 1990, and 370,000 today. In 2025, 66 percent of new homes and 43 percent of used homes on the market were HOAs. While HOAs are not the only reason for home cost increases, they contribute to being a significant barrier for young people who want to buy homes. Mortgages are harder to get when HOA fees are calculated into the borrower's debt-to-income ratio.

---

3. Henry George, *Progress and Poverty*.

An unethical practice by localities is "home equity theft." This occurs when a locality seizes a home for failure to pay property taxes, sells the home, and then keeps the entire proceeds. Fortunately, a Supreme Court decision (Tyler v. Hennepin County, 2023) has declared this a violation of the takings clause in the Fifth Amendment. About a dozen states engaged in this practice. Some states have begun amending their laws.

Home ownership is an important aspect of economic autonomy. It has been part of the "American Dream," and a natural desire for secure, dependable shelter that one can design to personal tastes.

## Conclusion

An integral economy should seek to tax economic transactions and avoid taxing existing assets and wealth. The public seizure of wealth beyond what is owed is unethical. Land and other commons involve fees or taxes for administration directly tied to land and infrastructure developed by cities or HOAs. When people buy homes in towns or HOAs, they agree to these terms. Henry George's position of taxing the community land commons value, but not the buildings or improvements, fits our integral economic framework.

The increased cost of homes, taxes, HOA fees, and insurance creates an entry barrier to home ownership that impedes the path to economic autonomy for young families and creates an incentive to delay having children. In an integral society, the economic path upward for everyone should be improved, not restricted, and economic institutions, personal and impersonal, should facilitate home ownership.

# Chapter 10

## An Economic Path Upward

In an integral economy, all individuals need an economic path upward for their pursuit of happiness. On the right, families, schools, and communities should educate and socialize an individual through personal relations. The goal is to produce a productive moral agent who attains economic autonomy and engages in positive, productive relations within society. On the left, impersonal institutions should provide a framework that allows individuals the freedom to develop. They might help facilitate this process, but certainly not block the path upward for any individual.

In previous chapters, we explained how the banking system, corporate taxation, and patents are used in ways that create obstacles to an individual's upward economic path. Systemic reforms are required to level the economic playing field, allow everyone to profit from both their labor and capital, and provide a framework for the distribution of corporate profits to shareholders. These reforms can remove major obstacles to an integral economy.

In this chapter, we discuss the development of human capital, the creation of the agency and autonomy an individual needs to be a competent and productive player in society, with a focus on the economic capacity to care for oneself and serve others.

Personal institutions on the right create productive and self-sufficient moral agents. This involves stages of psychosocial development and how individuals can successfully complete them. The most concise description of these stages that lead individuals to an integral life is Erik Erikson's eight stages of psychosocial development.

## Erik Erikson's Eight Stages of Development

**Figure 7. Erik Erikson's Eight Stages of Psychosocial Development**[1]

| Stage | Age Range (Approximate) | Psychosocial Crisis | Basic Virtue / Strength | Description |
|---|---|---|---|---|
| 1 | Birth to 18 months | Trust vs. Mistrust | Hope | Infants learn to trust caregivers for consistent care;<br>failure leads to fear and mistrust of the world. |
| 2 | 18 months to 3 years | Autonomy vs. Shame & Doubt | Will | Toddlers develop independence (e.g. toilet training exploration);<br>success builds self-control failure leads to shame. |
| 3 | 3 to 5 years | Initiative vs. Guilt | Purpose | Children take initiative in play and activities;<br>success fosters purpose excessive guilt can inhibit exploration. |
| 4 | 6 to 11 years | Industry vs. Inferiority | Competence | School-age children focus on skill-building and productivity; success builds competence<br>failure leads to feelings of inferiority. |
| 5 | 12 to 18 years | Identity vs. Role Confusion | Fidelity | Adolescents explore who they are and their beliefs/values;<br>success leads to a coherent identity<br>failure causes confusion. |
| 6 | 18 to 40 years | Intimacy vs. Isolation | Love | Young adults form close committed relationships;<br>success brings intimacy<br>failure leads to loneliness and isolation. |
| 7 | 40 to 65 years | Generativity vs. Stagnation | Care | Middle-aged adults contribute to society and guide the next generation (e.g. parenting mentoring);<br>success fosters care<br>failure leads to stagnation. |
| 8 | 65 years and older | Integrity vs. Despair | Wisdom | Older adults reflect on life; success brings acceptance and wisdom<br>failure results in regret and despair. |

**Figure** 7 lists the eight stages of development. At each stage, the individual faces a crisis that needs to be successfully resolved. Each stage

1. Erikson, E. H. (1950). *Childhood and Society.* New York: W. W. Norton.

builds on the previous ones, so an unresolved crisis can lead to dysfunction at later stages.

Studies have examined how different cultures address these stages: Chinese vs. Western, Native American, etc. Child-rearing practices, rites of passage, and collectivist vs. individualist cultures yield different results. Yet these stages persist due to the spontaneous biological and social nature of human life. Erikson thought there was a co-evolution of these stages alongside technological and other societal developments.

For an integral economy, productivity and competence, ages 2 to 11, are very significant stages. Failure to pass these stages might lead to a life of social dependency, crime, and a loss of economic value to society. There is an important cultural link to these basic virtues that can prove disastrous when experiencing conflicting cultures and ideologies.

## Cultural Dislocation and Intergenerational Change

Erikson studied American Indian tribes and the culture whose economy depended on buffalo as a resource.[2] The slaughter of the buffalo and people's placement on reservations caused cultural trauma, loss of agency, and apathy among the children. Immigration to the United States from other cultures can also cause trauma in children and dysfunction in adults. It is important that primary caregivers, facilitators, and schools provide a psychosocial bridge that can enable the formation of economic purpose and competence in the new society.

Celebration and affirmation of their former food, customs, and dance might help immigrants feel accepted, but are inadequate for providing meaningful and productive psychosocial adaptation—success in the eight stages in the new social environment.

This problem also exists intergenerationally, as new technologies like the internet, smartphones, and AI upset traditional cultural work and education patterns. Jonathan Haidt has done extensive study of how parenting habits and school expectations have significantly failed to prepare children for a productive and happy adult life in the age of

---

2. Ibid. Chapter "Hunters Across the Prairie."

the smartphone. He uses the catchy phrase "prepare the children for the road, not the road for the children."[3] Affirmations like "you are OK as you are," or asking children what they want, do not provide the guidance needed to progress through Erikson's stages. "Coddling" led to bad school curricula, acting up, bullying, increased teen suicide (especially in girls), guilt, a false sense of entitlement, and a host of other failures of psychosocial development.

The impact of the internet and smartphones is as culturally traumatic in our day as the printing press and the proliferation of ideas in books and pamphlets during the Renaissance and Reformation. Children born after 1995 tend to have more problems in environments designed for pre-internet life. Adjustments are needed when initial attempts fail. Societies might take different paths to reach the same destination: producing a productive moral agent who can pursue happiness and serve others at the same time.

Psychosocial maldevelopement cannot be solely blamed on either the right or the left, the parents or government schools. Old social institutions are maladapted to new social developments. This includes both families and schools. Families can adapt more quickly because of personal relationships rooted in love. Schools and government institutions lag further behind because they have bureaucratic inertia, as rules, employees, and teachers were shaped by the previous generation.

## Welfare Dependency

Modern welfare systems were well-intentioned but have structural problems and perverse incentives that cause dependency, inhibit psychosocial development, promote bureaucratic expansion, and are economically unsustainable in the long term. Unlike families and churches that are motivated by personal relationships and finances to help individuals become independent and self-sufficient, the federal government "headcount" payments foster welfare dependency that becomes intergenerational.

3. Greg Lukianoff and Jonathan Haidt, *The Coddling of the American Mind,* (NY: Penguin Press, 2018), p. 237ff.

This problem dates back to the New Deal Aid to Dependent Children (ADC) federal matching grant system. The federal government reimbursed states an open-ended share of expenditures. More recipients caused more federal dollars to flow automatically. These payments became considered a legal right. States had little incentive to remove people from welfare, as that would reduce federal funds. They also became dependents.

In 1961, amendments included federal reimbursement for foster care placements, ADC-Foster (AFDC). States were paid per child when they removed children from "unsuitable" homes and qualified for AFDC. In 1980, the Adoption Assistance and Child Welfare Act paid states per eligible child in out-of-home care. This created a perverse incentive for states to remove children from parents rather than maintain families.

Other programs like Medicaid (1965) used the same per-enrollee reimbursement model. States receive federal matching for every qualifying person added to the rolls. This is called the headcount model. It provides states with perverse incentives to keep people in the system. Agencies receive more reimbursements the longer someone stays in foster care, group homes, or on rolls. They discourage self-sufficiency, prolong foster placements, and reduce family reunification and job placements. Recipients become stuck in a "welfare trap" when leaving the program and starting a low-end job means losing benefits and making life more economically difficult.

Headcount funding fuels administrative growth. Agencies expand staff for eligibility determinations, case management, oversight, and paperwork to process and justify caseloads to receive more federal matching dollars. Administrative growth often outpaces caseload growth. The welfare bureaucracy today oversees more than 80 means-tested programs that collectively cost over $1 trillion annually, with significant overhead for compliance, audits, and reporting. Agency heads become empire builders, seeking larger budgets and more political influence.

Federal funds to serve individuals go to support more overhead costs. Moral hazard and increased fraud occur as payments for individuals get sent to fraudulent providers. When states become sanctuaries for "illegals," they bill the federal government for services and expand state bureaucracies, causing federal payments to balloon. This system is unsustainable. These "entitlements" first crowd out funding for other federal expenses, such as infrastructure and security. Next, they threaten more ethical payments like Social Security insurance. Finally, they can lead to federal bankruptcy.

More ethical welfare systems with better psychosocial outcomes need to be free of headcount payments. (The more you pay for something, the more of it you get.) Can impersonal governments implement systems that provide the personal development that families and churches have provided, without large numbers of people falling through the cracks, as they did before the 1930s?

## Babylonian and Roman Approaches

Babylonian and Roman civilizations were organized differently, but they had to provide some safety nets and give people an economic path upwards. No matter how a society is organized, what its religious beliefs are, it will have refugees, immigrants, orphans, widows, and the sick who cannot care for themselves or have the skills to succeed in society.

### Mesopotamia

Temples in ancient Babylon and broader Mesopotamia functioned as major economic and social institutions. They were large, self-sustaining agricultural estates that combined religious duties to care for vulnerable groups—widows, orphans, the poor, and refugees—with a practical welfare approach that contributed to economic autonomy.

Communal living and economic productivity were functions of these temples. Temples owned vast irrigated farmland, workshops, and animal herds. Residents who were able to work farmed, herded, practiced trades like pottery, weaving, metalworking, cooking, brewing, and selling surpluses in markets. Temples were often started with grants of irrigated land from kings and then became self-funded. Religious donations helped those who could not work. They were independent and productive religious and economic institutions that provided a safety net and welfare without any "headcount" drain on state funds.

Temples also served as paths to economic independence, especially for adult-age orphans and displaced people who wanted their own homes and families. Residents learned marketable skills at the temple and could keep some money from sales of their products. Successful individuals transitioned to private households, small farms, or trades. Many were integrated into the broader society and made room for others in the temple.[4]

The temple system was a reliable social safety net that sought to make people economically independent, much like personal traditional family/church models in the West. This system did not create a bloated bureaucratic rentier class to manage, regulate, and audit government welfare payments. This system functioned sustainably for approximately 1500 years, from 2000-500 B.C.

## Rome

Rome did not have a welfare system as integral as Babylon, but many people found an economic path upward through a patronage system, in which wealthier "patrons" provided support in exchange for loyalty and labor. The patron gained labor/services and prestige, while the client gained security and opportunities. It was somewhat like an apprenticeship, but not limited to trades or timetables, and might involve becoming a member of the household. It was an informal, decentralized, incentive-aligned support system.

Rome also had more formal apprenticeships for crafts and trades, where young people aged 12-15 would work, and perhaps live with, a master craftsman for a set period of time to master a trade.

Rome also had slaves, often people captured from foreign lands. For many, slavery was also an economic path upward, especially in urban areas. Freeing a slave was considered a virtuous act, showing mercy, generosity,

4. Gwendolyn Leick, *The Babylonians: An Introduction* (New York: Routledge, 2003), pp. 75-79.

and civic-mindedness, and serving as a reward for loyalty. Many slaves were treated more like patrons. This is very different from stereotypes of slavery in the South in the United States, where slaves were treated more like economic tools than human beings, although it was more like that in rural agricultural areas.

While manumission (freeing a slave) was a decision of the slave holder and varied by region, inscriptions on graves indicate that nearly 60 percent of slaves who had graves were freed by age 30, and 90 percent in total. Many freed slaves could marry and have families before they were beyond childbearing age. In urban areas, many slaves were freed after 5-6 years,[5] whereas agricultural slaves were held longer—10-20 years.[6]

Many Roman slaves had a better economic path upward than Americans caught in a welfare trap. It isn't a model because some masters could be cruel, and some slaves were never freed. But urban slave holders, concerned about their prestige and reputation in society, provided a decent economic path upward for most of their slaves.

In Rome, the centralized distribution of grain and food as welfare and/or a reward for political voting was problematic. It was the result of political pandering for votes. This led to idleness for some Roman citizens, satisfied to live off the free food rather than work productively. Politicians eventually resorted to extortion and heavy threats on farmers to keep the free food flowing. They levied higher taxes and exploited provinces to pay for the large quantities of grain. This was unsustainable, drained the treasury, and caused emperors to dilute the gold and silver in coins, much like fiat money printing today.

Unlike the Babylonian temple system, Roman incentives for production and psychosocial development were disconnected from political policies, with politicians providing free stuff for votes. Historians consider this a factor, not the entire cause, of the collapse of the Roman Empire.

---

5. Wiedemann, T.E.J. "The Regularity of Manumission at Rome." The Classical Quarterly 35, no. 1 (1985): 162–175.

6. Walter Scheidel, "Quantifying the Sources of Slaves in the Early Roman Empire," *Journal of Roman Studies,* 1997.

## A Structural Path Upward

While the headcount welfare system in the United States and other Western societies provides subsistence, it is inefficient, economically unsustainable, and disconnected from providing individuals an economic path upward. Both the Babylonian and Roman societies developed an economic path upward for many individuals in need of training or welfare. There were personal institutions. But slavery existed alongside these paths.

In Babylon, self-supporting temple communities provided a safety net and skills for people to transition to a self-sufficient and rewarding life. The Romans had a patronage system that enabled young people to serve as protégés or apprentices, learning life skills and trades while reinforcing other elements of Erikson's eight stages of psychosocial development. Both these systems were based on personal relations.

When state policies in Rome provided food handouts for votes, inefficiency, lethargy, free-riding, fraud, and financial collapse followed. This parallels the failures of welfare systems in the West today. It is a mistake to think that impersonal state institutions can provide the personal education required to create a productive worker.

The first warning signs of the AFDC program's failed approach came from Daniel Patrick Moynihan, who served as Assistant Secretary of Labor. He showed that, historically, families were poor when the husband was unemployed, but beginning around 1960, as more fathers were employed, AFDC payments also went up. Benefits were structured around father absence. The system financially rewards family breakdown, and this impacts the children's opportunity to pass through the stages of psychosocial development.[7]

The 1996 Personal Responsibility and Work Opportunity Reconciliation Act (PRWORA) tried to fix this. It replaced the AFDC federal headcount model with Temporary Assistance for Needy Families

7. Daniel Patrick Moynihan, *The Negro Family: The Case for National Action* (Washington, DC: Office of Policy Planning and Research, United States Department of Labor, March 1965), 5–6.

(TANF) block grants. This capped federal funding, and states had to use the funds more judiciously. This drove national caseloads down about 60 percent in the following decade. However, Title IV-E foster care, Medicaid, and similar programs remained open-ended entitlements, preserving the headcount dynamic in child welfare and health services. While most states rationed resources, the headcount system created flawed and unsustainable incentives.

Illinois, Tennessee, and Oklahoma adopted strategies that rewarded providers for successfully getting people employed and out of the system. Successful examples are few but helpful. Generally, impersonal state institutions (on the left) need to provide contracts to personal institutions (on the right). They are paid when people successfully leave the system and do not return. This can be tied to a separate form of minimum safety net, but needs to avoid welfare traps.

At the federal level, programs can support personal-level development from lessons learned from the communal programs in Babylon or the patronage system in Rome. This involves 2-3 years of service at a low wage in exchange for gaining skills for future self-autonomy. Such programs should not leave graduates debt-ridden like some federal student loan programs trap students today.

One successful program that does this is veterans' benefits. After military service of 2-4 years, which helps develop self-discipline and loyalty to society, veterans can receive free college tuition and a guaranteed no-down-payment home loan. On average, veterans have higher levels of employment, income, and home ownership—more economic autonomy—than non-veterans. It would be socially beneficial to have a parallel civil service program for other government agencies, from city and county to state and federal levels.

## Youth Civil Service Program

The military is not the only government agency that provides services to society. Most government jobs are considered "civil service" positions. A significant number of civil service jobs are routine bureaucratic tasks or manual labor work that can be quickly learned from their predecessors with a few weeks' overlap on the job. Many positions cost society a lot of money when filled by highly-paid union workers who receive generous pensions. Youth civil service employees could do these jobs as well in return for minimum wages, college tuition, and home-loan guarantees, saving all governments money over the long term.

A government agency could net lifetime savings of $1-3 million per position over 45 years.[8] This is a win-win-win scenario for the youth civil servant, the agency, and the taxpayer. Of course, agencies would still need some career professionals, as the military does. This varies in the military, with the Marines needing fewer careerists, while the Air Force requires more. On average, about 50% of the military is made up of people who serve less than six years.

We propose that the economy would become more integral by addressing the needs of psychosocial development for all youth by creating an economic path upwards through a Youth Civil Service and Economic Autonomy Act. A draft bill for this purpose is proposed in Appendix 4.[9] This proposal is intended to provide a smooth transition for youth into the labor market.

## Baby Bonds And Wealth Distribution

In our binary economy, we also need to consider an opportunity for everyone to have opportunities in the capital market. Large student loan debt has led people to propose other strategies to help young people avoid that trap. While the Youth Civil Service Act addresses that problem, there is still a need for everyone to access capital income in our binary economy where capital generates a large percentage of the production of economic goods.

Some redistribution schemes, like the $1,000 per month universal basic income (UBI) proposal by Andrew Yang in his 2020 presidential

8. See Section 2 (a)(7) in Appendix 4.

9. This Act was prepared by Grok/X-AI based on the parameters and principles provided for a youth civil service program.

bid, provide perverse economic incentives. By now, the reader should understand that such cash transfers would be problematic, like head-count welfare systems or Rome's grain distribution. They cause inflation, idleness, and economic collapse. We got a glimpse of this in the massive inflation caused by COVID-19 checks given to replace income for productive work and business with idleness.

Both Democrats and Republicans have proposed "baby bonds." These bonds are government-created investment accounts for children when they are born. After age 18, they would be able to draw on this capital for college or a first home, as our Youth Civil Service program would do. One of these proposals passed in 2025, branded "Trump Accounts." Three alternatives exist, but none provide a significant capital income stream for the poor or provide a clear path to widespread distribution of future capital income.

### The American Opportunity Accounts Act

The American Opportunity Accounts Act (AOAA), sponsored by Democratic Senator Cory Booker in 2019, and again in 2024, would deposit $1,000 into a baby bonds account for each newborn and add annually an amount up to $2,000 based on a sliding family income scale. These bonds would be interest-bearing U.S. Treasury securities. One simulation argued:

> Without baby bonds, we project the median white family would have $300,000 in financial wealth in 2042–46, while the median Black family would have $126,000 and the median Hispanic family $125,000. With baby bonds, the median white family wealth increased slightly, to $310,000, while the median wealth for Black and Hispanic families increased more significantly, to $148,000 and $165,000, respectively. That represents a decrease in the wealth gap.[10]

---

10. Damir Cosic, Madeline Brown, Amalie Zinn, Sonia Torres Rodríguez, and Ofronama Biu, *Modeling the Impact of a Federal Baby Bonds Program: Impacts on Financial Wealth, College Attainment, Student Debt, Home Equity, and Retirement Savings,* (urban.org) December 5, 2024. https://www.urban.org/research/publication/modeling-impact-federal-baby-bonds-program

This proposal is funded by U.S. securities, with ongoing appropriations from the general fund. Revenue to pay for this would (1) reduce the minimum cap on inheritance taxes from 15 million to 3.5 million, (2) raise the percentage of the tax from 40 percent to 45 percent, (3) close the step-up reset gap, and (4) raise the capital gains tax to 28%. The first three items would transfer increased wealth from the deceased to the newborn poor. A lump-sum amount from securities plus interest, restricted to education and home loans, is turned over at age 18.

The yield of treasuries is far less than capital investments in other baby bond proposals. The interest is about the same as inflation. Because these bonds are not capital investments, they do not contribute to the growth of the economy. Recipients can use the funds to get a head start as wage earners, but they are not set up for a future capital income stream. This proposal fails to recognize the essence of the binary economy and fails to provide a greater share of capital ownership in corporate shares to the next generation. There is no plan for the baby to have a capital income stream from economic production.

## The Connecticut Baby Bonds Trust

In 2021, Connecticut became the first state to create baby bond accounts. Connecticut accounts are for children of low-income families on Medicaid. The Connecticut Treasurer deposits $3,200 into an account managed by the state until age 18. These are put in the state's investment accounts and are expected to be between $10,000 and $24,000 at age 18. This can be spent between ages 18 and 30 for in-state uses: getting an education, buying a home, or starting a business in Connecticut.

Connecticut's program does not suffer from the AOAA's ongoing revenue necessity because it is prefunded. It does not put the state budget at risk, nor does it directly transfer wealth as an inheritance tax. It is funded by capital income from mixed investments in bonds and productive capital. To the extent they are invested in productive capital, they contribute to economic growth and carry associated risks.

Because Connecticut's funds must be spent in the state before age 30, they incentivize the individual to remain in the state and contribute to its economy. It compensates for Connecticut parents unable to help their children get an education, buy a home, or start a business. However, individuals are required to remain in a very expensive state. Further, capital accounts are not turned over so that they can be used as seeding lifelong investment accounts for a capital income stream. Like the AOAA, these bonds assume the bondholder will earn a living from labor.

### Invest America Act (Trump Accounts)

Senator Ted Cruz's Invest America Act framework was branded as the Trump Accounts in the 2025 Big Beautiful Bill. These accounts provide a one-time $1,000 federal seed for all children born 2025–2028 and create tax-deferred investment accounts to which others, like family members or philanthropists, can contribute.

The government does not manage these accounts, which are opened by parents or guardians. It adds the $1,000 seed for eligible births and allows additional contributions up to $5,000 per year. These funds must be managed by private firms in low-cost U.S. equity index funds, such as the S&P 500, with fees capped at 0.10 percent. This directly exposes accounts to capital markets and compound stock-market growth, while minimizing the risks of investing in single corporations.

They provide every child the same start, with no government bias towards the poor, as the AOAA or Connecticut bonds. However, wealthy individuals and philanthropists can contribute specifically to accounts for disadvantaged children, helping close the wealth gap voluntarily.

The Invest America Act specifically invests in the productive economy. Cruz and other backers emphasize that children will gain financial literacy, and this type of bond will lead to an "ownership society." There is risk, but "a rising tide lifts all boats." We all sink or swim together.

The tax deferrals on capital gains mean the government might eventually get some of its seed money back through taxes. The government benefits from investments in productive companies along with the account holders if the funds generate profits. Unlike the AOAA, which has to contribute to accounts every year, the Invest America Accounts end up costing the federal government very little. The one-time $1,000 seed money invested into the S&P 500 with returns at the rate of the last 10-year average would be about $11,000. Voluntary contributions would significantly increase this amount. The government might get the original $1,000 back through deferred taxation. Wealthy people will fund their children's accounts more than poor children, so there is no structural mechanism that will significantly close the capital income gap.

At 18, these accounts are used like the other baby bonds: for education, a home down payment, or a business startup. They do not produce a capital income stream, as a binary economic perspective would recommend. High school graduates receive more of a start in the labor market than the capital market. Apart from the seed money, account contributions come from investment returns or private contributions, not the government.

### CESJ's Capital Homestead / Capital Ownership Accounts

The Center for Economic and Social Justice (CESJ) goes beyond other baby bond programs by advocating lifetime capital accounts with some similarities to an IRA. CESJ is inspired by Louis Kelso's binary economics.

The specific innovation is a democratized form of capital credit placed in accounts at birth, like baby accounts. This credit is issued by the government at low interest, like the Federal Reserve's discount window for corresponding banks. This credit is used to buy newly issued, full-voting, full-dividend-payout shares in growing private companies. The loans are repaid entirely over time by the dividends and capital gains. Upon repayment from capital earnings, the account owner has a capital account that generates income that can be used for anything, including retirement.

CESJ proposes some systemic reforms related to corporate taxes and dividends that differ from our Shareholder Dividend and Corporate Tax Reform Act, but share the same purpose. The goal is more widespread capital ownership, a lifetime capital income stream, and a more democratized capital income stream without redistributing any existing wealth. CESJ calls this approach "the just third way":

> There is an alternative that is neither socialism nor capitalism. This "just third way" would be a free enterprise economy, generating private sector profits — but with ownership of the new growth systematically flowing to every individual citizen.[11]

Capital Homestead Accounts are still theoretical and in an advocacy stage. Like Trump Accounts, they grow from investment in productive markets, tied to the development of the economy and cost the government little or nothing. And, like Trump Accounts, taxes are deferred, providing some income tax revenue when resources are pulled from the accounts. However, unlike Trump Accounts, they provide a capital revenue stream that can grow over time for the life of the account holder. This democratizes income from capital and can greatly reduce government welfare expenses.

### Shareholder Dividend and Corporate Tax Reform Act

Except for the AOAA, all the above Baby Bond or government trust accounts would benefit from our Shareholder Dividend and Corporate Tax Reform Act (Appendix 2). The Connecticut accounts and Trump Accounts would see higher dividend returns on their portfolios invested in productive companies. And the Capital Homestead Accounts could be simplified because many of the systemic reforms CESJ is proposing would no longer be necessary.

While dividends would be tax-deferred, delaying government tax revenues as the system phased in, higher dividend payouts would lead to higher personal tax payments that would offset the loss of corporate income taxes.

11. Center for Social and Economic Justice, "The Economic Democracy Act: A Plan for Getting Ownership, Income, and Power to Every Citizen" https://www.cesj.org/learn/economic-democracy-act/plan-for-getting-ownership-income-and-power-to-every-citizen/

## The Capital Income Act

We propose the Capital Income Act[12] (Appendix 5), which is an innovative hybrid that takes the best elements of existing baby bonds/Trump Accounts and layers on a CESJ/binary economics-style capital credit mechanism. The focus is on lifetime income from capital, rather than preparation for the labor force with lump-sum disbursements to young adults. Everyone has an opportunity to develop a capital income stream.

Our Youth Civil Service and Economic Autonomy Act already provides a backstop for youth joining the labor force. It provides greater benefits in terms of health and education than current baby bonds approaches, while reducing government labor and pension costs.

The Capital Income Act does more. It complements wage labor income, with a democratized capital income stream. It is integral economic evolution based on concepts developed in this book.

At birth, when a new Social Security number is assigned, the U.S. Treasury would automatically open a "Capital Credit Account" in the child's name and provide $10,000 in government capital credit. This is not a grant like Trump Accounts, but an interest-free seed capital loan in the name of the child, but controlled by the Treasury until it is repaid from future earnings. This requires no permanent capital outlay, except for the devaluation due to inflation, as the seed money remains property of the Treasury.

The account is invested in low-cost S&P 500-style index funds like the Trump Account investment strategy, maximizing average gain and minimizing risk. Contributions can be added by parents, the individual, or others up to $5,000 per year, tax-deferred, like Trump Accounts. At age 18, an automatic repayment and ownership transfer is triggered. The Treasury withdraws the original $10,000 credit and transfers ownership of the account to the individual. A projection of the average account balance would be $45,600 if no additional contributions were made. Although this amount depends on market performance and would have

12. The Capital Income Act (Appendix 5) was drafted by Grox X/AI based on parameters we provided.

only a 4 percent chance of being less than $10,000 at maturity, we believe the $45,000 figure to be overly conservative if the Shareholder Dividend and Corporate Tax Reform Act were also passed and significantly more dividends were contributed to the returns.

After age 18, the account becomes the individual's personal, tax-advantaged vehicle, like an IRA. Investment income is not taxed until withdrawn, creating the possibility of a lifetime stream of capital income to supplement wages. Withdrawals are flexible. In short, every 18-year-old will receive capital accounts like the trust fund babies of the wealthy—maybe not as large, but significantly larger than other plans, significantly democratizing capital ownership in the country.

Capital income accounts shift the baby bond emphasis from "preparation for labor income" to a possibility of a lifetime stream of income from capital and a binary income, complementing the labor income support from the Youth Civil Service Act.

## Conclusion

This chapter focuses on three aspects of an economic path upward for all: (1) the psychosocial development of individuals and their self-autonomy before entering onto the playing field of society; (2) the institutional reforms that create an ethical framework for that economic path upward; and (3) structures that initiate both labor and capital market opportunities for young people.

Policies of impersonal institutions tend to treat people as abstract units rather than individuals at a particular stage of psychosocial development. When institutions do not consider an individual's upward economic path, well-intentioned programs to provide a safety net often turn into welfare traps. There are important life markers like birth, high school graduation, and retirement, where impersonal governments can act integrally to provide baby trust accounts, civil service accounts, safety nets, and guardrails that enable an upward economic path without causing exploitation or welfare traps.

Examples from Babylon, Rome, and the G.I. Bill show ethical

alternatives to "headcount" systems that create welfare traps, bloated bureaucracy, and fail to promote individuals' psychosocial development or economic autonomy. We propose policy reforms that will serve an economic path upward in a binary economy: the Shareholder Dividend and Corporate Tax Reform Act (Appendix 2), the Youth Civil Service and Economic Autonomy Act (Appendix 4), and the Capital Income Act (Appendix 5).

# Chapter 11

## An Economic Reformation

This book lays out a path for an economic reformation comparable to the protestant reformation in religion. Control of money is taken from central banks and economic institutions and given to the people, as modern republics distributed power from kings to the people through representatives and a vote. The economic reformation is partial, because when the United States was founded, people had economic autonomy and democracy based on their labor value as farmers or tradesmen. Capitalism enables far greater prosperity, but has been centralized. We need a Capitalist Reformation

### An Economic Reformation

The Catholic Church and the Pope promoted a unified top-down cultural institution, and the Kings of the Holy Roman Empire had governed with their sword. The capitalist system that arose among wealthy industrialists and government-controlled central banks concentrated economic power in the hands of the few who controlled capital income distribution.

A powerful backlash was spearheaded by Marx and Engels in the *Communist Manifesto.* While they recognized injustice, they created a more centralized and economically dysfunctional system. The Communist Party deprived everyone of the ownership of capital. The Party pushed an aberrant form of psychosocial development that failed to pass Erikson's stage four, industry vs. inferiority. Neither the institutions Marx critiqued, nor the institutions that followed in his footsteps, were able to turn the ownership of the capitalist economy over to the people. The world today is divided between these two unethical economic frameworks.

One hundred years after Marx, Louis Kelso and Mortimer Adler wrote *The Capitalist Manifesto,* which outlined a theory of binary economics recognizing the importance of everyone owning and earning income from capital in addition to their labor. This insight requires a transformation of our social and economic institutions from serving the minority to serving everyone and a bottom-up spontaneous economic order.

This book describes an integral economic framework in which society stands stable on three pillars: impersonal social institutions (the left wing), personal institutions (the right wing), and integral consciousness (the head). In this social framework, neither the right nor left fights to control the other: both have a role to play. The right puts responsible economic agents on the field; the left frames the field and referees ethical rules. Both wings are informed by an integral social consciousness in the "head."

Institutions that make up the ethical framework of society do not control individuals through central planning. They serve the plans of individuals in their pursuit of life, liberty, and happiness as facilitators and referees. The individuals who are "players" in society are not free to do anything their lizard brain urges, but should behave as responsible people producing, exchanging, loving, caring, and serving others as Erickson's stages of psychosocial development describe.[1]

Relationships are the essence of society. When individuals and institutions embody an integral consciousness in relationships, society will develop sustainably, and individuals will be happy.

## Macro-Economic Reforms

The reforms we describe and the proposed bills we have attached as appendices are macro-level economic reforms. They describe major changes that shift the ownership and control of capital from central institutional

1. See Figure 7, Chapter 10.

control to individuals. We discussed structural principles and individual motivations. We have described objective ethical frameworks that make economic institutions facilitators and referees. Individuals are described as subjective economic actors pursuing an upward economic path. This is the engine of a productive, sustainable, and socially evolutionary economy.

The reforms proposed include the ownership of money. The central bank should be transformed from an owner to a central ledger system in a decentralized economy based on the people's assets and activities. Current central economic institutions are transformed from players to referees. The Decentralized Banking and Currency Stability Act we propose (Appendix 1) does for the economy what the separation of church and state did for religion.

Taxes need major reforms, with an emphasis on taxing relationships rather than institutions, people, or things. If you tax one of the three legs that hold up society, you weaken its support system. However, if you tax transactions within society—income from labor or capital, a sales tax on a product, or a tariff on imports—taxes become voluntary and not an act of theft, which weakens a leg of the economy.

We have suggested several tax reforms to make the entire system more functional and integral. The most critical is the widespread distribution of income on capital made possible by the Shareholder Dividend and Corporate Tax Reform Act proposed in Appendix 2. This removes the government from being an interloper in the production process, making corporations dysfunctional, and looting the capital income that should go to shareholders, the true owners, who, in turn, are taxed on capital income the same as labor income.

Patent reform is also needed. The U.S. founders wanted patents to serve economic development, but Congress inadequately developed an ethical framework in patent law. Monopolistic price gouging and patent shelving to avoid production were not desired by the founders. These problems become more serious when patents are held by objective institutions rather than subjective individuals with a moral conscience. Our Patent Reform and Public Access Act (Appendix 3) proposes legislation that would promote innovation by rewarding the patent holder with a windfall without enabling monopoly control or shelving of patents.

Our final macro reforms concern economic welfare and an upward path toward economic autonomy for all individuals. We examined the failures of headcount welfare systems, beginning with ADC, and how these failures lead to welfare traps, bloated bureaucracies, and systemic economic collapse. They incentivize dependency, idleness, and meaninglessness, rather than incentives, purpose, productivity, and happiness. While traditional families and churches provide personal attention and these virtues, some impersonal public support can help those who fall through the cracks, whether from broken homes or social dislocation. Governments can contribute to personal autonomy not by throwing money at agencies based on headcounts, but by supporting personal institutions like families and communities that enable people to contribute to society.

In our study of the economic paths upward in Babylonian and Roman societies, we discovered that these systems had some superior elements to current welfare systems. The Babylonian temples and the Roman patronage system were successful personal institutions. However, this represented a right-wing-only approach. There were no left-wing guardrails to prevent slavery that kept people trapped.

We discussed expanding military veteran benefit programs that provide an economic path upward, including 2-4 years of civil service in lower-skilled government jobs at minimum wage in exchange for educational and housing benefits like the GI Bill. At the same time, government budgets for agencies can be reduced. The Youth Civil Service and Economic Autonomy Act (Appendix 4) proposed to do this.

Then we explained that the Youth Civil Service and Economic Autonomy Act would better accomplish the goals of the current government baby bonds and trust programs. However, there is a need to create permanent capital income streams for everyone in the binary economy described by Kelso and Adler in *The Capitalist Manifesto.*

We noted the pioneering work done by the Center for Economic and Social Justice (CESJ) on the creation of Capital Homestead or Ownership

Accounts. All individuals, not just "trust fund babies" of wealthy individuals, should have a capital ownership stream. Thus, we propose the Capital Income Act that combines features of Trump Accounts with a substantially greater contribution from capital credit accounts against future production established by the Department of the Treasury. These capital accounts could enable every child, including those born in poverty, to become trust fund babies of the entire economy. Our proposed Shareholder Dividend and Corporate Tax Reform Act amplifies the returns in these accounts, leading to a golden age for all.

Many microeconomic reforms, such as in healthcare and specific areas, can make further improvements. These are topics for other books or policy papers. Our presentation has provided the macroeconomic reforms and principles to help make other policy decisions more integral and economically functional.

We have described a general framework where an integral economy, like a stool, rests solidly on three legs (or two wings and a head); ethical economic institutions, economically responsible individuals, and an evolving historical social consciousness. The five bills proposed in the book would create an economic reformation, transforming centrally controlled economic institutions into economic institutions enabling the spontaneous economic order that best serves individuals and society as a whole. This is no less evolutionary than the Protestant Reformation combined with the institutional separation of church and state.

# Appendices

# Appendix 1: Decentralized Banking and Currency Stability Act

## Decentralized Banking and Currency Stability Act[1]

**A BILL**

To establish a decentralized banking system in which private banks bear the risks and rewards of lending, to limit currency issuance to objective rules tied to broad-based family economic conditions, to eliminate too-big-to-fail institutions through size and diversification limits, to phase in a Central Ledger Authority and phase out the Federal Reserve gradually over seven years so as to avoid disruption to the existing financial system, and for other purposes.

**Be it enacted by the Senate and House of Representatives of the United States of America in Congress assembled,**

**SECTION 1. SHORT TITLE; TABLE OF CONTENTS.**

(a) Short Title.—This Act may be cited as the "Decentralized Banking and Currency Stability Act of 2026".

(b) Table of Contents.—[Omitted for brevity; sections follow in order.]

**SECTION 2. FINDINGS AND PURPOSE.**

(a) Congress finds that—

(1) the current centralized monetary system concentrates power and risk in a single institution and enables too-big-to-fail dynamics;

(2) a decentralized system in which private banks compete, can fail, hold meaningful reserves, and are subject to hard size and diversification limits better aligns incentives with long-term stability and broad individual prosperity;

1. This Act was prepared by Grok/X-AI based on the parameters and principles provided for an integral banking system.

(3) currency creation must be strictly rule-based and tied to verifiable growth in the number of households and real median household income to prevent inflation, deflation, and elite capture while accommodating family housing and productive business expansion; and

(4) any reform must include a multi-year phase-in to preserve the continuity of credit, payments, and deposit insurance.

(b) **Purpose.**—The purpose of this Act is to—

(1) replace the Federal Reserve's discretionary money-creation and reserve-holding functions with a transparent Central Ledger Authority that performs only accounting and rule-enforcement duties;

(2) require private banks to operate under a 35 percent reserve requirement, strict productive-lending standards, a national deposit cap, and single-borrower limits;

(3) cap annual net currency issuance according to an automatic formula based on Census Bureau data; and

(4) implement these changes gradually over seven years with appropriate grandfathering and safety valves.

**SECTION 3. DEFINITIONS.**

In this Act:

(1) **Central Ledger Authority** or **CLA** means the independent office established under section 4.

(2) **Corresponding Bank** means any FDIC-insured depository institution that maintains accounts on the Master Ledger and engages in fractional-reserve lending.

(3) **Productive Lending** means loans originated for the creation or expansion of tangible productive assets, including family-owned housing, business fixed investment, commercial and industrial capacity expansion, and infrastructure that directly serves household needs. Loans for government transfer payments, military procurement

unrelated to productive assets, or purely financial speculation do not qualify.

(4) **Master Ledger** means the centralized, public, real-time digital ledger maintained by the CLA recording all corresponding-bank deposits, loans, and currency balances.

(5) **Real Median Household Income** means the inflation-adjusted (C-CPI-U) median household income published annually by the Bureau of the Census in the Current Population Survey Annual Social and Economic Supplement.

## SECTION 4. ESTABLISHMENT OF THE CENTRAL LEDGER AUTHORITY.

(a) The Board of Governors of the Federal Reserve System is redesignated as the Central Ledger Authority.

(b) The CLA shall—

(1) maintain the Master Ledger;

(2) issue new currency only to corresponding banks up to the annual cap established in section 7;

(3) destroy currency returned upon loan repayment; and

(4) have no authority to hold assets, make loans, conduct open-market operations, or set interest rates.

(c) All non-monetary supervisory and regulatory functions of the former Federal Reserve shall transfer to the Office of the Comptroller of the Currency, the Federal Deposit Insurance Corporation, and the Consumer Financial Protection Bureau as appropriate.

## SECTION 5. RESERVE REQUIREMENTS FOR CORRESPONDING BANKS.

(a) Requirement.—Each corresponding bank shall maintain reserves equal to not less than 35 percent of its transaction and nonpersonal time deposits.

(b) Phase-In.—The requirement shall be phased in linearly over seven years beginning January 1, 2027, as follows:

- Year 1 (2027): 5 percent
- Year 2 (2028): 10 percent
- Year 3 (2029): 15 percent
- Year 4 (2030): 20 percent
- Year 5 (2031): 25 percent
- Year 6 (2032): 30 percent
- Year 7 (2033) and thereafter: 35 percent.

(c) Existing deposits and loans as of December 31, 2026, are grandfathered and shall not be subject to the new reserve calculation until their natural maturity or rollover.

(d) Failure to meet the phased requirement shall result in automatic restrictions on new lending until compliance is restored.

**SECTION 6. BANK SIZE AND DIVERSIFICATION REQUIREMENTS.**

(a) **National Deposit Cap.**—No corresponding bank may hold more than 2 percent of total national insured deposits (measured annually by the CLA using the most recent FDIC Summary of Deposits data).

(b) Single-Borrower Lending Limit.—No corresponding bank may extend loans or credit to any single borrower (or group of related borrowers) exceeding 8 percent of its total outstanding loans.

(c) **Phase-In Schedule.**—The requirements shall be phased in linearly over seven years beginning January 1, 2027, as follows:

- Year 1 (2027): Deposit cap = 14.29 percent; Single-borrower limit = 14.29 percent of total loans
- Year 2 (2028): Deposit cap = 12.57 percent; Single-borrower limit = 12.57 percent of total loans
- Year 3 (2029): Deposit cap = 10.86 percent; Single-borrower limit = 10.86 percent of total loans
- Year 4 (2030): Deposit cap = 9.14 percent; Single-borrower limit = 9.14 percent of total loans
- Year 5 (2031): Deposit cap = 7.43 percent; Single-borrower limit

= 7.43 percent of total loans

- Year 6 (2032): Deposit cap = 5.71 percent; Single-borrower limit = 5.71 percent of total loans
- Year 7 (2033) and thereafter: Deposit cap = 2 percent; Single-borrower limit = 8 percent of total loans.

(d) **Grandfathering and Compliance.**—Existing deposits and loans as of December 31, 2026, are grandfathered until natural maturity or rollover. Banks exceeding the phased caps may not grow beyond their current share until compliant; the CLA shall publish annual compliance reports on the public dashboard.

(e) **No Shock Clause.**—If the CLA determines (using objective metrics published in advance) that the phase-in of sections 5 or 6 is causing measurable credit contraction exceeding 2 percent of GDP in any year, the scheduled tightening for that year shall be halved and deferred to the following year.

**SECTION 7. RULE-BASED ANNUAL CURRENCY CAP.**

(a) **Formula.**—On or before January 15 of each year, the CLA shall publish the maximum allowable net new currency issuance for that calendar year according to:

**Annual Currency Cap ( percent) =** $H_{t-1} + M_{t-1} + B$

where—

- $H_{t-1}$ = verified annual percentage growth in the total number of U.S. households (Census Bureau Housing Vacancies and Homeownership survey or Current Population Survey);
- $M_{t-1}$ = verified annual percentage growth in real median household income (Census Bureau CPS ASEC);
- $B = 0.3$ percent (fixed stability buffer).

If the calculated cap is negative, it shall be floored at zero percent.

(b) **Enforcement.**—The CLA shall limit aggregate new currency issuance across all corresponding banks to the cap applied to the prior year-end currency stock. All data and calculations shall be published in real time on a public dashboard.

(c) **Transitional Cap (2027–2029).**—For the first three years, the cap shall be the greater of the formula above or 3.0 percent, to ensure continuity during phase-in.

(d) **Triennial Median Net Worth Safeguard.**—Concurrent with each release of the Federal Reserve Survey of Consumer Finances, if real median family net worth has stagnated or declined (≤ 0 percent growth) for two consecutive three-year periods, the annual cap for the following three years shall be reduced by an additional 0.5 percentage points.

**SECTION 8. PRODUCTIVE-LENDING REQUIREMENT AND LOAN-RETENTION RULE.**

(a) New loans funded by currency issued under the cap may be made only for productive lending as defined in section 3.

(b) Each originating bank shall retain at least 50 percent (or the full term, whichever is shorter) of every loan it originates for a minimum of five years. Securitization or sale before this period is prohibited except in FDIC-supervised resolution.

(c) Non-productive government expenditures shall be financed solely through transparent congressional appropriations and taxation; no corresponding bank may lend for such purposes.

**SECTION 9. DEPOSIT INSURANCE AND BANK FAILURE PROTECTIONS.**

(a) All corresponding banks must be FDIC-insured. The FDIC shall continue to administer the Deposit Insurance Fund exactly as under current law.

(b) In the event of bank failure, depositors are protected up to the statutory limit; the failed bank's assets are resolved by the FDIC without recourse to the CLA or new currency issuance.

**SECTION 10. TRANSITION PROVISIONS.**

(a) **Grandfathering.**—All existing Federal Reserve notes, deposits, and loans as of the date of enactment remain fully valid and enforceable.

(b) **Fed Balance-Sheet Wind-Down.**—The existing Federal Reserve balance sheet shall be allowed to mature naturally over ten years; no new asset purchases are permitted after enactment. Any residual assets after ten years shall be transferred to the Treasury for debt reduction.

(c) **Payments-System Continuity.**—The CLA shall maintain the existing Fedwire, ACH, and other payment rails without interruption.

(d) **Regulatory Relief During Phase-In.**—Banks in compliance with the phased reserve and diversification schedules shall be exempt from any new stress-test or capital rules that conflict with this Act until full implementation in 2033.

(e) **No Shock Clause.**—If, in any year during the phase-in, the CLA determines (by objective metrics published in advance) that the transition is causing measurable credit contraction exceeding 2 percent of GDP, the reserve increase or diversification tightening for that year shall be halved and the shortfall deferred to the following year.

## SECTION 11. REPEALS AND CONFORMING AMENDMENTS.

(a) Sections 19(b) and 28 of the Federal Reserve Act (12 U.S.C. 461, 463) concerning discretionary reserve requirements and open-market operations are repealed effective upon full phase-in.

(b) All references in Federal law to "Federal Reserve Notes" shall be deemed to mean currency issued under this Act.

(c) Technical and conforming amendments to titles 12 and 31, United States Code, shall be made as necessary by the Office of the Law Revision Counsel.

## SECTION 12. EFFECTIVE DATE.

This Act shall take effect on January 1, 2027, except that sections 4 and 10 (establishing the CLA and transition rules) shall take effect on the date of enactment.

## SECTION 13. SEVERABILITY.

If any provision of this Act is held invalid, the remainder shall not be affected.

**END OF BILL**

# Appendix 2: Shareholder Dividend and Corporate Tax Reform Act

## Shareholder Dividend and Corporate Tax Reform Act[1]

**A BILL**

To eliminate the corporate income tax, require minimum dividend distributions to shareholders, mandate public trading for large corporations, and promote broader economic participation through capital income.

**Be it enacted by the Senate and House of Representatives of the United States of America in Congress assembled,**

**SECTION 1. SHORT TITLE; TABLE OF CONTENTS.**

(a) **Short Title.**—This Act may be cited as the "Shareholder Dividend and Corporate Tax Reform Act of 2026".

(b) **Table of Contents.**—[Standard table omitted for brevity]

**SECTION 2. FINDINGS AND PURPOSE.**

Congress finds the following:

(1) The corporate income tax imposes significant compliance costs exceeding $126 billion annually and distorts business decisions away from productive investment.

(2) Forcing a minimum cash return to shareholders respects shareholder equity, provides predictable personal income (especially for lower- and middle-income households), and generates steady federal revenue through ordinary income taxation.

(3) Requiring large corporations to be publicly traded expands investment opportunities and reduces wealth concentration in private entities.

1. This Bill was prepared by Grok/X-AI based on the parameters and principles provided for an integral corporation system.

(4) The purpose of this Act is to eliminate entity-level corporate taxation, mandate a minimum dividend floor while preserving flexibility for higher distributions, and adapt the corporate form to an economy in which capital returns increasingly supplement or displace labor income.

**SECTION 3. REPEAL OF CORPORATE INCOME TAX.**

(a) **Repeal.**—Section 11 of the Internal Revenue Code of 1986 is repealed.

(b) **Phase-In.**—For taxable years beginning—

(1) in 2027, the tax imposed by section 11 shall be 10 percent;
(2) after December 31, 2027, the tax imposed by section 11 shall be zero.

(c) **Conforming Amendments.**—The Secretary of the Treasury shall make all necessary conforming amendments to the Internal Revenue Code, including the repeal or modification of related provisions (e.g., alternative minimum tax for corporations, foreign tax credit rules).

**SECTION 4. MANDATORY MINIMUM DIVIDEND DISTRIBUTIONS.**

(a) **New Section.**—Subchapter C of chapter 1 of the Internal Revenue Code of 1986 is amended by adding at the end the following new section:

**"§ 306. Mandatory minimum dividend distributions"**

"(a) **General Rule.**—Every corporation with taxable income (determined under this title, applying generally accepted accounting principles with adjustments prescribed by the Secretary) shall distribute as a cash dividend not less than the applicable percentage of such income to its shareholders of record on the last day of the taxable year."

"(b) **Applicable Percentage.**—For taxable years beginning—

(1) in 2027, 10 percent;
(2) in 2028, 20 percent;
(3) after December 31, 2028, 30 percent.

"(c) **Higher Distributions Permitted.**—Nothing in this section shall prohibit or limit a corporation from distributing any amount greater than the minimum required.

"(d) **Anti-Avoidance.**—The Secretary shall prescribe rules preventing the avoidance of this requirement through controlled groups, subsidiaries, recharacterization of distributions, or artificial reserves.

"(e) **Dividends Taxed as Ordinary Income.**—Any distribution required or made under this section shall be included in the gross income of the recipient shareholder and taxed at the rates applicable to ordinary income under section 1 (wage and salary income rates)."

(b) **Effective Date.**—The amendment made by this section shall apply to taxable years beginning after December 31, 2026.

## SECTION 5. PUBLIC TRADING REQUIREMENT FOR LARGE CORPORATIONS.

(a) Amendment to Securities Exchange Act of 1934.—Section 12 of the Securities Exchange Act of 1934 is amended by adding at the end the following new subsection:

"(m) **Mandatory Registration for Large Corporations.**—

"(1) Any corporation (including any controlled group) with average annual gross receipts exceeding $5,000,000,000 for the 3 preceding taxable years shall register its equity securities under this section and become a reporting company on a national securities exchange within the phase-in period.

"(2) Phase-In.—Corporations meeting the threshold as of the date of enactment shall comply by December 31 of the following years:

2028: 25 percent of required public float;

2029: 50 percent;

2030: 75 percent;

2031 and thereafter: 100 percent (minimum public float of 25 percent of outstanding shares).

"(3) The Securities and Exchange Commission shall issue rules to facilitate broad retail and institutional participation, including simplified listing standards and encouragement of low-minimum investment vehicles."

(b) **Coordination with IRS.**—The Secretary of the Treasury and the SEC shall jointly issue regulations to prevent circumvention through restructuring or foreign entities.

**SECTION 6. REGULATORY BROADENING OF OWNERSHIP.**

The SEC shall, within 18 months of enactment, promulgate rules requiring covered public companies to maintain at least 25 percent public float and to offer simplified access (e.g., fractional shares, low-fee index products) to encourage participation by lower- and middle-income investors.

**SECTION 7. EFFECTIVE DATES; TRANSITION RULES; REVENUE NEUTRALITY.**

(a) Except as otherwise provided, this Act applies to taxable years and periods beginning after December 31, 2026.

(b) The Secretary and the SEC may issue transition relief for corporations demonstrating good-faith compliance difficulties.

(c) The Congressional Budget Office and Joint Committee on Taxation shall prepare a revenue estimate; any net revenue loss shall be offset through future adjustments if necessary, consistent with the goal of steady personal-income-tax collections.

**SECTION 8. SEVERABILITY.**

If any provision is held invalid, the remainder shall not be affected.

# Appendix 3: Patent Reform and Public Access Act

## Patent Reform and Public Access Act[1]

**A BILL**

To promote the progress of science and the useful arts by replacing exclusive patent monopolies with a compulsory royalty licensing system, to ensure reasonable compensation to inventors while preventing price gouging, to provide taxpayers a fair return on federally funded research, and for other purposes.

**Be it enacted by the Senate and House of Representatives of the United States of America in Congress assembled,**

**SECTION 1. SHORT TITLE; TABLE OF CONTENTS.**

(a) Short Title.—This Act may be cited as the "Patent Reform and Public Access Act of 2026".

(b) Table of Contents.—[Omitted for brevity in this draft.]

**SECTION 2. FINDINGS AND PURPOSE.**

(a) Congress finds that—

(1) Article I, Section 8, Clause 8 of the Constitution empowers Congress to secure exclusive rights to inventors for limited times to promote progress, but does not require that such rights create an absolute monopoly that permits unchecked price gouging;

(2) the current exclusive-patent system, while incentivizing innovation, has led to excessive pricing in critical sectors such as pharmaceuticals and medical devices;

1. This Act was prepared by Grok/X-AI based on the parameters and principles provided for patent reform..

(3) federally funded research (through grants from agencies such as the National Institutes of Health, National Science Foundation, or National Aeronautics and Space Administration) has produced many inventions that are later commercialized under exclusive patents, causing taxpayers to pay twice—once for the research and again through monopoly pricing;

(4) during the COVID-19 pandemic, the United States government invested billions of dollars through Operation Warp Speed, BARDA, and NIH grants to accelerate mRNA vaccine development and manufacturing; Moderna received substantial direct federal R&D funding, and the underlying platform benefited from decades of public research, yet the resulting patented vaccines were sold to the government at approximately $15–$37 per dose (with bivalent boosters around $26–$30) before transitioning to commercial prices; both companies announced plans to charge $110–$130 per dose for boosters in the private market, while independent analyses estimated manufacturing costs at only $1–$3 per dose and Medicare reimbursement rates for adult booster doses reached approximately $156–$162; this generated tens of billions in private revenue while limiting broader access and returning little direct value to taxpayers; and

(5) a compulsory royalty system will maintain strong incentives for inventors, enable immediate competition to lower prices, and ensure a predictable return to both inventors and the public.

(b) **Purpose.**—The purpose of this Act is to—

(1) establish a uniform 10 percent royalty-based compulsory licensing regime for all utility patents;

(2) fix the government's share of royalties in advance when a federal grant is awarded, regardless of the actual percentage of costs ultimately attributable to the grant; and

(3) simplify accounting and reporting through existing IRS information-return forms while providing dedicated funding and streamlined

regulatory pathways to prevent approval bottlenecks at the Food and Drug Administration.

## SECTION 3. COMPULSORY ROYALTY LICENSING.

Title 35, United States Code, is amended by inserting after chapter 29 the following new chapter:

### "CHAPTER 30—COMPULSORY ROYALTY LICENSING"

**§ 301. Right to use patented invention upon payment of royalty.**

(a) **General Rule.**—Notwithstanding any other provision of this title, any person may make, use, offer to sell, sell, or import into the United States any invention claimed in a patent issued under this title, provided that such person pays to the patent owner (or the patent owner's assignee) a royalty equal to 10 percent of net sales of the product embodying the patented invention.

(b) **Net Sales Defined.**—For purposes of this section, "net sales" means gross receipts from sales minus returns, rebates, and applicable taxes, as determined under standard accounting principles.

(c) **No Injunction; No Treble Damages.**—No court may issue an injunction to prevent use authorized under subsection (a), and no enhanced damages under section 284 shall apply to such use.

(d) **Applicability.**—This section applies to any utility patent issued on or after the date of enactment of this Act. Existing patents remain subject to pre-enactment law until expiration.

**§ 302. Payment and enforcement of royalties.**

(a) Royalties shall be paid quarterly.

(b) The patent owner may bring a civil action in a United States district court solely to recover unpaid royalties plus interest at the statutory rate; no injunctive relief or exclusion from the market shall be available.

## SECTION 4. GOVERNMENT SHARE FOR FEDERALLY FUNDED INVENTIONS.

(a) **Amendment to Bayh-Dole Act.**—Section 202 of the Bayh-Dole Act (35 U.S.C. § 202) is amended by adding at the end the following new subsection: "

**(f) Compulsory Royalty Share for Federally Funded Inventions.**—

(1) Any grant agreement, cooperative agreement, or contract awarded by a Federal agency that may result in a subject invention shall include a clause specifying a fixed percentage (the 'Government Royalty Percentage') of any royalties received by the contractor or grantee under section 301 of title 35.

(2) The Government Royalty Percentage shall be determined and fixed at the time the grant is awarded and shall be based on the ratio of the Federal award amount to the total projected R&D budget for the project (or such other reasonable formula as the agency may establish by regulation). **Once fixed, the percentage shall not be adjusted or re-determined based on actual costs incurred or actual Federal contribution realized.** This fixed-percentage approach provides agencies flexibility when funding high-risk or high-development-cost projects.

(3) The contractor or grantee shall include a flow-down provision in any license or assignment requiring the licensee to pay the Government Royalty Percentage directly to the funding agency (or its designee) as a portion of the 10 percent royalty required under section 301.

(4) The Government's share shall be deposited in the general fund of the Treasury and may be used, subject to appropriation, to support further scientific research."

(b) **Applicability.**—This section applies to all grant agreements executed on or after the date of enactment of this Act.

## SECTION 5. REPORTING AND ACCOUNTING SIMPLIFICATION.

(a) **Mandatory Information Returns.**—Any person who pays royalties under section 301 (a "sub-rights holder") shall file with the patent owner and with the relevant Federal funding agency (if a Government Royalty Percentage applies) an information return on IRS Form 1099-MISC (or any successor form designated for royalty payments) reporting the total royalties paid during the calendar year.

(b) **Timing and Penalties.**—Returns shall be furnished on or before January 31 of the year following the payment year, in accordance with existing IRS rules for Form 1099-MISC. Failure to file shall be subject to the penalties provided in sections 6721 and 6722 of the Internal Revenue Code of 1986.

(c) **Centralized Collection Option.**—The Secretary of the Treasury, in consultation with the Director of the United States Patent and Trademark Office, may establish a centralized electronic portal for sub-rights holders to submit Form 1099-MISC filings and remit the Government's share directly, further simplifying accounting for all parties.

## SECTION 6. FDA REVIEW FUNDING AND STREAMLINED APPROVAL PATHWAYS.

(a) **Additional Royalty for FDA Review.**—In addition to the 10 percent royalty required under section 301, any person who makes, uses, offers to sell, sells, or imports a patented invention that is a drug, biologic, or medical device subject to approval under the Federal Food, Drug, and Cosmetic Act or the Public Health Service Act shall pay an additional 2 percent of net sales (the "FDA Review Fee") to the Secretary of Health and Human Services.

(b) **Use of Funds.**—All FDA Review Fees collected shall be deposited into a dedicated "Compulsory Licensing Review Fund" and shall be available to the Food and Drug Administration, without further appropriation, solely for the purpose of expediting reviews, inspections, and approvals of products manufactured under section 301.

(c) **Streamlined Approval.**—The Secretary shall establish, by regulation within 180 days of enactment, an expedited "Compulsory License

Supplement" pathway that—

(1) permits reference to the data in the original New Drug Application, Biologics License Application, or device premarket approval;

(2) requires demonstration only of bioequivalence, manufacturing compliance, and labeling consistency; and

(3) targets review and approval within 6 to 10 months of a complete filing.

(d) **Applicability.**—This section applies only to human drugs, biologics, and medical devices; it does not apply to other utility patents.

**SECTION 7. SAVINGS PROVISIONS; REGULATIONS.**

(a) Nothing in this Act shall be construed to limit the Government's existing royalty-free license under section 202(c)(4) of the Bayh-Dole Act or its rights under 28 U.S.C. § 1498.

(b) The Director of the United States Patent and Trademark Office and the heads of Federal funding agencies shall issue implementing regulations within 180 days after the date of enactment.

(c) This Act shall not apply to design patents or plant patents.

**SECTION 8. EFFECTIVE DATE.**

This Act shall take effect on the date of enactment and shall apply to patents issued on or after that date and to grant agreements executed on or after that date.

**End of Draft Bill**

# Appendix 4: Youth Civil Service and Economic Autonomy Act

**Youth Civil Service and Economic Autonomy Act**[1]

**A BILL**

To establish the Youth Civil Service Corps as a civilian counterpart to the GI Bill, providing high school graduates a structured path of public service in exchange for postsecondary education and homeownership assistance, while reducing long-term government payroll costs and welfare dependency.

**Be it enacted by the Senate and House of Representatives of the United States of America in Congress assembled,**

**SECTION 1. SHORT TITLE.**

This Act may be cited as the "Youth Civil Service and Economic Autonomy Act of 2026" (or "Youth GI Bill Act").

**SECTION 2. FINDINGS AND PURPOSE.**

(a) **Findings.**—Congress finds the following:

(1) Many high school graduates lack the financial resources for immediate postsecondary education or training, leading to delayed economic autonomy, underemployment, or reliance on means-tested welfare programs.

(2) Government agencies incur high costs for routine but essential "drudgery" tasks (road maintenance, driver licensing and vehicle registration processing, administrative support) due to permanent staff salaries, benefits, and retirement obligations.

(3) A voluntary civil service program modeled on the post-World

1. This Act was prepared by Grok/X-AI based on the parameters and principles provided for a youth civil service program.

War II GI Bill can provide a reliable safety net, build skills and work ethic, and deliver clear pathways to independence while generating net savings through lower payroll expenses and reduced future welfare outlays.

(4) Historical models, including ancient temple-based communal labor and Roman patronage systems, demonstrate that tying temporary support to productive service and post-service benefits promotes self-sufficiency without fostering dependency.

(5) The 1965 Moynihan Report exposed how open-ended welfare programs with headcount-based funding can create perverse incentives that undermine family structure and long-term self-sufficiency.

(6) Evidence from the GI Bill and veteran outcomes demonstrates the effectiveness of structured national service. Post-9/11 veterans consistently outperform non-veterans in employment metrics: veterans had a 3.0% unemployment rate in 2024 compared to 3.9% for non-veterans. Veterans who use GI Bill benefits show 78% employment within two years of completing education (versus 64% for comparable non-veterans), enjoy an average annual earnings premium of approximately $5,000, and achieve significantly higher homeownership rates (76–79% versus ~60% for similar non-veteran cohorts). These outcomes confirm that combining temporary service with meaningful post-service educational and housing benefits produces superior long-term economic autonomy and reduced reliance on public assistance.

(7) Significant cost savings will accrue to government agencies. Using Youth Civil Service Corps participants at minimum wage plus health coverage for routine positions, instead of permanent unionized or civil-service employees, produces major net savings. Over a 45-year period covering one full-time equivalent position, approximately 15 youth participants (3 years each) cost roughly $2.76 million (service wages + education benefits), compared to $3–5+ million or more for a single permanent employee's salary, benefits, and lifetime pension.

These savings more than offset the education investment while reducing long-term payroll and retirement liabilities.

(8) Existing national service programs have shown strong returns on investment through participant earnings gains and societal benefits; expanding them with GI Bill-level rewards and targeted government staffing will amplify these outcomes.

(b) **Purpose.**—The purpose of this Act is to—

(1) establish a voluntary Youth Civil Service Corps for recent high school graduates;

(2) assign participants to essential but routine government functions at minimum wage plus health coverage;

(3) provide post-service educational benefits and home loan guarantees calibrated to service length; and

(4) achieve net fiscal savings by offsetting program costs with reductions in permanent government payroll, benefits, and long-term welfare expenditures.

## SECTION 3. DEFINITIONS.

In this Act:

(1) **Corps** means the Youth Civil Service Corps established under section 4.

(2) **Participant** means an individual enrolled in the Corps.

(3) **Qualifying service** means full-time service in approved government positions under the Corps.

(4) **Secretary** means the Secretary of Labor (or designee), in coordination with the Secretaries of Transportation, Homeland Security, and other relevant agencies.

## SECTION 4. ESTABLISHMENT OF THE YOUTH CIVIL SERVICE CORPS.

(a) The Secretary of Labor shall establish the Youth Civil Service Corps as a voluntary national service program administered through partnerships with Federal, State, and local government agencies.

(b) The Corps shall prioritize assignments in high-need areas such as:

(1) Infrastructure maintenance and road repair;

(2) Licensing, registration, and related administrative processing;

(3) Other essential but routine government office or field tasks in agencies with jobs that could be filled by high school graduates.

(c) Gradual Replacement of Positions.—The Corps is intended to achieve long-term cost savings by gradually replacing permanent employees in eligible routine positions through natural attrition. Agencies may fill vacancies resulting from retirements, resignations, contract expirations, or other voluntary separations with Youth Civil Service Corps participants. The Corps shall not be used to immediately displace or terminate current employees. Agencies shall develop and submit to the Secretary a five-year phase-in plan that—

(1) respects all existing collective bargaining agreements;

(2) prioritizes filling positions only as they become vacant; and

(3) demonstrates projected net payroll and pension savings.

(d) Training of Replacements.—Participants shall be required to train their replacements during a six-week overlap period at the end of their service term. This includes hands-on mentoring, documenting procedures, and ensuring smooth continuity of operations. Agencies shall incorporate this succession planning into program guidelines to maximize knowledge transfer and long-term efficiency gains.

**SECTION 5. ELIGIBILITY AND ENROLLMENT.**

(a) Eligible individuals are U.S. citizens or lawful permanent residents who—

(1) have received a high school diploma or equivalent;

(2) are between the ages of 18 and 24 at enrollment; and

(3) are not currently enrolled in postsecondary education or training.

(b) Enrollment is voluntary and competitive; preference given to those demonstrating financial need or barriers to college/trade school.

(c) Maximum term: 36 months (3 years). Participants may elect 24 months (2 years) with adjusted benefits.

**SECTION 6. COMPENSATION AND BENEFITS DURING SERVICE.**

(a) Participants shall receive—

(1) compensation at the Federal minimum wage (or the applicable State minimum wage, whichever is higher); and

(2) employer-sponsored health insurance coverage equivalent to entry-level Federal employee plans.

(b) Service counts toward Social Security credits and provides deferment/forbearance on any existing student loans.

(c) The Corps shall provide training, mentorship, and skill certification in areas such as infrastructure, administration, and civic leadership.

**SECTION 7. POST-SERVICE BENEFITS.**

(a) **Educational Benefits.**—

(1) Upon completion of 36 months of qualifying service: A voucher covering full tuition, fees, and a living stipend (modeled on Post-9/11 GI Bill rates) for up to 36 months of approved college or university education.

(2) Upon completion of 24 months of qualifying service: A voucher for up to 24 months of approved trade school, vocational, or certificate programs.

(b) **Home Loan Guarantee.**—Participants who complete their full term shall receive a no-down-payment home loan guarantee through the Department of Veterans Affairs or a designated Federal housing agency, on terms comparable to the VA home loan program (for primary residence purchase).

(c) Benefits are portable and may be used at any accredited institution or approved program.

**SECTION 8. FUNDING, COST OFFSETS, AND OVERSIGHT.**

(a) **Authorization of Appropriations.**—There are authorized to be appropriated such sums as may be necessary to carry out this Act for fiscal years 2027 through 2032.

(b) **Cost-Offset Requirement.**—Agencies utilizing Corps participants shall demonstrate annual net savings in payroll and benefits (by using minimum-wage temporary labor for routine tasks instead of permanent hires) and reduced future welfare expenditures attributable to higher participant earnings and homeownership rates. Savings shall be reinvested in the Corps or returned to the Treasury.

(c) **Performance Metrics.**—The Secretary shall track and publicly report:

(1) completion rates;

(2) post-service employment, earnings, and postsecondary attainment;

(3) documented government cost savings from staffing efficiencies and training of replacements; and

(4) reduction in welfare program utilization among participants.

(d) The Government Accountability Office shall conduct an independent evaluation after 5 years, with authority to recommend adjustments or termination if net savings are not achieved.

**SECTION 9. EFFECTIVE DATE.**

This Act shall take effect 180 days after the date of enactment.

# Appendix 5: Capital Income Act

**Draft — Capital Income Act**

**A BILL**

To establish Capital Income Accounts that provide every American child with a self-sustaining lifetime stream of capital income through market-based ownership of productive assets.

**SECTION 1. SHORT TITLE.**

This Act may be cited as the "Capital Income Act of 2026".

**SECTION 2. FINDINGS AND PURPOSE.**

Congress finds the following:

(1) Broadening direct ownership of productive capital is essential to long-term economic security, reducing reliance on labor income alone, and creating widespread opportunity in a high-productivity economy.

(2) Under reasonable long-term market assumptions (approximately 10 percent nominal annual total return on a broad S&P 500 index fund), the $10,000 initial capital credit provided at birth would grow on average to approximately $55,600 by age 18 from the seed alone. After the Treasury withdraws the original $10,000 credit, the individual would on average receive about $45,600 net attributable to the government seed at age 18.

(3) If the individual leaves the original seed and its growth untouched until age 30 before beginning to draw capital income, the seed alone would on average grow to approximately $174,500. This balance could prudently support an initial average annual capital income stream of roughly $7,000 per year (using a conservative 4% withdrawal rate that allows the principal to continue growing with the market).

(4) If the individual begins drawing capital income at age 35, the seed

alone would on average grow to approximately $281,000, supporting an initial average annual capital income stream of roughly $11,200 per year.

(5) If the full balance (including the seed and any additional contributions) is left invested until age 60 for retirement, the original $10,000 seed alone would on average grow to approximately $3.04 million, supporting an initial average annual capital income stream of roughly $122,000 per year, generating a substantial lifetime supplement without any reduction in current wages or consumption.

(6) This Act creates a universal, self-liquidating capital credit mechanism that gives every child an ownership stake in the U.S. economy from birth while minimizing long-term fiscal cost to taxpayers.

The purpose of this Act is to democratize access to capital ownership so that every American can build a personal stream of capital income to supplement wages, support families, and enhance retirement security.

### SECTION 3. CAPITAL INCOME ACCOUNTS.

(a) **Establishment.**—The Secretary of the Treasury shall establish a Capital Income Account in the name of every U.S. citizen born on or after January 1, 2027.

(b) **Initial Capital Credit.**—At birth, the Treasury shall credit each account with $10,000 in the form of a non-recourse capital credit.

(c) **Investment.**—The account shall be invested in low-cost, broad-based U.S. equity index funds that track the S&P 500 (or successor broad market index), with total annual fees not to exceed 0.10 percent.

(d) **Additional Contributions.**—Any individual (parent, guardian, or the account holder after age 18) may contribute up to $5,000 per year (inflation-adjusted) on a tax-deferred basis, treated similarly to a traditional IRA.

(e) **Transfer at Age 18.**—On the date the account holder attains age 18—

(1) the Treasury shall withdraw exactly $10,000 (the original capital credit); and

(2) full legal ownership of the remaining balance shall automatically transfer to the individual.

This transfer occurs regardless of the account balance.

(f) **Tax Treatment.—**

(1) Earnings within the account are tax-deferred.

(2) After transfer, the account shall be treated as a tax-advantaged individual retirement account under rules similar to section 408 of the Internal Revenue Code, with withdrawals taxed as ordinary income only when distributed.

(3) Contributions are not deductible, but growth and future income are sheltered until withdrawal.

**SECTION 4. ADMINISTRATION.**

The Secretary shall—

(1) contract with private custodians or fund providers for investment management;

(2) establish a secure online portal for account access and contributions; and

(3) issue annual statements to account holders.

**SECTION 5. EFFECTIVE DATE.**

This Act takes effect for all births occurring on or after January 1, 2027. This draft is ready for introduction (it can be expanded with technical amendments, CBO scoring language, or offsets if desired).

# Index

# About the Author

**Gordon L. Anderson** has a Ph.D. in Philosophy of Religion with a minor in International Relations from Claremont Graduate University. He developed a broad understanding of social systems working with Morton A. Kaplan, Distinguished University Professor at the University of Chicago. This included organizing major conferences on the Soviet System with Alexander Shtromas of the Hoover Institution (1985), the Chinese System with Ilpyong Kim of the University of Connecticut (1987), and Liberal Democratic Societies with Edward Shils of Cambridge University (1989).

As the President of Paragon House Publishers (1994- ), Anderson published a series of books on integral philosophy including writings by Ken Wilber, Allan Combs and Steve McIntosh. He also served as an adjunct professor at the California Institute of Integral Studies.

As Editor-in-Chief of *International Journal on World Peace* (1992-2021) Anderson edited many articles related to governance, the economy, and society. He focused on the problem of institutional capture after publishing the article "Institutional Value Theory and the Resiliency of Social Institutions," by Professor Don Trubshaw of the Department of Business at Nottingham Trent University. He studies binary economics and ideas for the just distribution of capital from Dr. Norman G. Kurland, President of the Center for Economic and Social Justice.

Anderson has practical experience with finance and governance as chair of the finance committee of the University of Bridgeport, and as President of the Legislative Evaluation Assembly of Minnesota. Before earning his Ph.D., Anderson earned a Degree in Mechanical Engineering from the University of Minnesota. As an engineer, he built test equipment for U.S. Navy nuclear submarines and the U.S. Space Shuttle. He is a Vietnam veteran, having served three years in the U.S. Army Signal Corps.